Collaborative Conversations Among Language Teacher Educators

Editors

Margaret (Maggie) Hawkins
Suzanne Irujo

Language Teacher Education Collaborative (LTEC)

Francis Bailey
Donald Freeman
Kathleen Graves
Margaret (Maggie) Hawkins
Suzanne Irujo
Diane Larsen-Freeman
Ellen Rintell
Jerri Willett

Typeset in Giovanni and Frutiger
by Capitol Communications Systems, Inc., Crofton, Maryland USA
and printed by Victor Graphics, Inc., Baltimore, Maryland USA

Teachers of English to Speakers of Other Languages, Inc.
700 South Washington Street, Suite 200
Alexandria, Virginia 22314 USA
Tel 703-836-0774 • Fax 703-836-6447 • E-mail publications@tesol.org •
http://www.tesol.org/

Director of Publishing: Paul Gibbs
Managing Editor: Marilyn Kupetz
Copy Editor: Craig Triplett
Additional Reader: Sarah Duffy
Cover Design: Capitol Communications Systems, Inc.

Chapter 1 contains text, conversation, and response from F. Bailey, M. Hawkins, S. Irujo, D. Larsen-Freeman, E. Rintell, and J. Willett, "Language Teacher Educators' Collaborative Conversations," *TESOL Quarterly*, 32, pp. 536–546. Used with permission.

The text section in chapter 4 is from D. Larsen-Freeman, "On the changing role of linguistics in the education of second-language teachers: Past, present, and future." In J. Alatis, C. Straehle, B. Gallenberger, and M. Ronkin (Eds.), *Georgetown University Round Table on Languages and Linguistics 1995* (pp. 722–723). Washington, DC: Georgetown University Press. Used with permission.

The text section in chapter 5 is excerpted from D. Freeman and K. Graves, *Reexamining language teachers' teaching knowledge: A conversation*. Paper presented at the 27th Annual TESOL Convention, April 1993, Atlanta, GA.

Every effort has been made to contact the copyright holders for permission to reprint borrowed material. TESOL regrets any oversights that may have occurred and will rectify them in future printings of this work.

ISBN 1-93118514X
Library of Congress Control No. 2004106807

To all reflective practitioners who struggle to better understand language learning and teaching.

Table of Contents

ACKNOWLEDGMENTS

This work would not have been possible without the help and encouragement of colleagues, families, and friends. Each member of the Language Teacher Education Collaborative has a list of people who should be acknowledged, but we will do that individually and personally. As a group, LTEC extends sincere gratitude to the following people:

To all the students and colleagues with whom we have collaborated over our long careers, for providing insights, feedback, and new ideas

To the six respondents whose thoughtful comments on our work appear in this book, for taking the time to engage with our conversations and provide a classroom perspective on our discussions

To Courtney Cazden and Julian Edge, for reading and responding to a very early version of our work

To the two anonymous reviewers, for their critical insights, and to Julian Edge, as chair of TESOL's Publications Committee, for helping us merge the reviewers' comments with our own strong opinions about what we wanted to do

To the editorial staff at TESOL, especially Craig Triplett, for helping make our meandering conversations and academic prose readable, and Marilyn Kupetz, for her care and efficiency in shepherding the book through the publication process.

Collaborative Reflection as Critical Practice in Teacher Education

Donald Freeman and Margaret (Maggie) Hawkins

Changes in Teacher Education

Teacher education is not what it used to be. The thinking and practices that have characterized teacher education and professional development programs are changing. The broad sweep of these changes has moved from focusing exclusively on how to do things in the classroom and why these technicist solutions work based on rationales drawn heavily from academic disciplines, to focusing on teachers' work as it evolves, as reasoning in action (Johnson, 1999) in the contexts of time, place, and individual history.

Following trends in education more generally, the preparation and professional development of all teachers has been transformed in the past decade. Zeichner (1999) described the dynamics of these changes in his 1998 vice-presidential address to the Division on Teaching and Teacher Education of the American Educational Research Association. In his address, titled "The New Scholarship in Teacher Education," he outlined how teacher education has moved from "discover[ing] the most efficient strategies for training teachers and prospective teachers to perform particular actions in classrooms" (p. 4), through a recognition of the importance of teachers' cognitive processes, to a more reflective and critical approach.

In English for speakers of other languages (ESOL), teacher education has followed a similar path. In their seminal volume, *Second Language Teacher Education* (1990), Richards and Nunan delineated ESOL teacher education as an area for research and theorizing in its own right. Since then, the research base has expanded as researchers have examined teacher learning in ESOL contexts (Freeman & Richards, 1996), and debates over the knowledge-base in ESOL teacher education (Freeman & Johnson, 1998; Yates & Muchisky, 2003) have addressed the relative primacy and balance of knowledge derived from academic disciplines, from participants' experience, and from teacher education more broadly.

At its core, this evolution represents a shift from emphasizing teacher education—the structures and processes through which individuals are prepared as teachers—to emphasizing teacher learning—the processes through which individuals learn and are socialized as teachers. Although these two approaches arguably serve the same purpose, they are not isomorphic. It is fair to say, to paraphrase Stevick's famous syllogism from *Teaching Language: A Way and Ways* (1980, p. 16), that there can be teacher learning without teacher education (as in teachers learning autonomously), but it would be difficult to claim that teachers were being educated unless teachers had learned something. Thus teacher learning—how teachers come to understand, analyze, and critique what they do—lies at the heart of this new focus. Referred to variously as *reflective teaching* (e.g., Richards & Lockhart, 1994) or *reflective practice* (e.g., Zeichner & Liston, 1996), this emphasis on teacher learning examines how individuals learn by engaging with their own teaching, their students, their context, and their professional roles as teachers.

Teacher learning can have internal and external dimensions that are closely linked. Reflective practice often refers to the internal dimension that calls for the individual teacher to engage in a close and disciplined examination of the processes and outcomes of his or her work (e.g., Ballenger, 1999; or in ESOL, Appel, 1995). *Critical reflection* refers to the external dimension that attends explicitly to how issues of class, gender, race, culture, and language affect teaching and learning in classrooms (e.g., Britzman, 1991; or in ESOL, Samuel, 1998). Often taken in tandem, these two approaches aim to foster in teachers a "self-reflexive and self-critical attitude" (Ramanathan, 2002, p. 146). While such self-study has not been common among teacher educators, Zeichner (1999) notes that "this work can both inform the practices of the teacher educators who conduct it and contribute to knowledge and understanding of teacher education for the larger community of scholars and educators" (p. 11).

Time, Structure, and Community

Teachers generally work in isolation. They spend much of their time in individual pursuits without the chance to confer or collaborate professionally with others: teaching in their classrooms, planning lessons, and communicating with their students. Opportunities to exchange ideas or discuss with colleagues what they know or believe are rare and valued. Most professional development fails to counteract such isolation. The chance to think together, in disciplined ways, through collaborative exploration, reflection, and conversation is key. Three elements—time, professional space, and disciplined ways of thinking (Teacher Knowledge Project, 2003)—make such interactions productive.

These elements have been constituted in a number of ways in professional development interactions. The literature has documented teachers engaging in reflective practice, either as individuals or in one-on-one collaboration with a teacher educator (e.g., Souza Lima, 1998; Macgillivray, 1997). These projects have yielded useful insights and have been disseminated through the traditional professional means, often replayed at a distance through journal articles and conference presentations. Other initiatives, which entail spontaneous conversations triggered by current situations, are more immediate and evanescent. Predicated on the belief that understandings and interpretations are constructed continuously through interaction, these approaches follow the sharing, challenging, and negotiating of meanings that occur moment-by-moment as teachers interact with knowledgeable others (e.g., Bailey, 1996; Hawkins, 2000; Willett & Miller, 2004).

Regardless of the tenor and occasion of such interactions, the role of talk is key. At their heart lies the ebb and flow of language, expression, and representation. Hollingsworth (1994) describes this dynamism in a teacher collaborative she worked with:

> Because of our ongoing relationship, the talk in our meetings did not usually take on the form of *dialog*—similar to the conversation in

a play or novel, which appears to have two or more voices, but which actually comes from one author's perspective. Nor was it simply a *discussion* of pre-arranged topics and readings through a formal discourse structure. Rather the collaborative and sustained *conversation* became the exchange and reformulation of ideas, intimate talk, and reconstructive questions. (p. 6)

For the talk to add up to something, the interaction needs a structure and a focus. There are numerous examples of such designs; we mention five here:

- *book talk* discussions in the Learning Community, a teacher education program in Hawaii in which student teachers met monthly for conversations, using books as catalysts to promote reflection on cultural issues (Florio-Ruane, 2001)
- *multicultural collaboratives* in four cities that brought together teams of teachers from different schools to explore critical education (Freedman, Simons, Kalnin, & Casareno, 1999)
- *teacher study groups* in which mainstream and ESL teachers examined English language learners' academic work as a way to improve their own performance (Clair, 1998)
- *cooperative groups* for faculty professional development (Edge, 2002)
- *exploratory teaching* in which teachers gather to examine "puzzles" in classroom practice (Allwright, 2003)

These efforts all have a predetermined structure (often rather loose) that allows the conversations to unfold and provides a focus to anchor them. For talk to be organized, time must be set aside, and people must come together. Thus these key elements of time and structure lead to and are reinforced by an emerging sense of professional community among participating teachers (Grossman, Wineburg, & Woolworth, 2001). Together these elements seem to provide an antidote to the chronic isolation and alienation that can encroach on practicing teachers.

The irony is that teacher educators usually do not address professional isolation any better than teachers do. They too lack time (often because they do not take it), an organized structure, and a group of colleagues with whom they can examine their work. As teacher educators, many of us promote such approaches for teachers and incorporate them into our teacher education practices. However, we often do not engage in such endeavors ourselves. Yet we, also, often live our daily professional lives in isolation, relying on a larger (and more geographically scattered) professional community to share information about the issues and practices that make up our work. And this information is often conveyed in print through professional papers or in formulaic conference presentations, which do not permit deep probing or lasting exchanges. Thus we deny ourselves rich opportunities to arrive at new or redefined understandings through sustained discursive interactions.

This book departs from that norm. It documents the efforts of one group of language teacher educators to create a local professional community within which we could critically reflect together on our work. We offer it not as a model or a formula but as a guided excursion into how we have thought about, questioned, and reformulated what we do as language teacher educators.

LTEC: Language Teachers Educational Collaborative

The Language Teachers Educational Collaborative (LTEC) was first convened by Maggie Hawkins and Jerri Willett at the University of Massachusetts at Amherst in June 1992. That first meeting sought to bring together a geographically proximate group of colleagues in ESOL teacher education from diverse institutions of higher education to explore common issues in our work. We did not know then where things might lead, whether we could find common ground among our various views and affiliations, or whether the conversations would gain enough momentum and interest to persevere in our time-choked work lives.

As the chapters of this book attest, the group not only survived but indeed flourished over the next 5 years. We met quarterly at first and then seasonally, in the fall, winter, and spring. Though a few members came and went, the core group that contributed to this book remained the same throughout. The venue rotated; the agenda and its processes evolved; but the contacts went on. How did such a loose, free-form professional group survive? What provided the basis for engagement? In an institutionally stratified work world where parochial concerns are often paramount and time is so pressured, how did this group of ESOL teacher educators continue to meet to digest and critique what they were doing? Why do it?

In a sense, this book tries to answer that question. The LTEC group's sporadic encounters offered participants the place and the discipline to examine and reexamine core issues in their work as ESOL teacher educators. LTEC meetings allowed us to step out of the day-to-day work of teaching and supervision, to stand back from the rhythm and assumptions of what we were doing, and to think about it. The actual process involved thoughtful, prepared conversation. These were not spontaneous sessions; we were not griping or brainstorming. Instead, the step-by-step agenda that evolved— reading a text prepared by one person, then spending time discussing that text and ultimately relating ideas from the discussion back to our individual work—gave our conversations form and discipline. Thus, following the framework described above, we provided a time, a professional space, and a structure within which disciplined ways of thinking could occur and be articulated and negotiated.

As members of the group became more familiar with one another, professional postures softened. People began to seek out contradictions and question each other's assumptions and boundaries. Why do you think this or that? How do you know? What is your evidence? Sometimes people shifted their ideas; sometimes they agreed to disagree. Generally, we resolved very little during these meetings. In fact, the meetings usually left a lot of unsettling loose ends. As informal as these interactions were in a professional sense, the meetings were neither confessional nor self-indulgent. Rather, they often served to push each individual's thinking, to identify and analyze intractable issues in courses we were teaching or with teacher learners with whom we were working as supervisors or advisers. To talk in this way, to be able to think deeply with colleagues about both specific and crosscutting issues in our work as teacher educators created a critical form of professional development that is rarely available to those who teach teachers.

Those of us who participated found the experience immensely valuable. The conversations, albeit sometimes messy and challenging, provided new insights and perspectives on our practices and our beliefs. They challenged and pushed us—not always a comfortable process. We found, at times, broad areas of mutual interest and concern, where the diversity of perspectives expanded our thinking. At other times, issues were raised that some of us had not considered and that forced us to squirm a bit as we critiqued our practices. We also had an ongoing debate about the group's membership: whether to keep a stable and familiar membership or to invite newcomers. Some felt that new participants would refresh the conversation by offering different views; others felt that part of the group's efficacy lay in our shared history, known relationships, and established foundational thinking.

At one point, after meeting for roughly 2 years, we felt a need to redefine the group's purpose and goals. That engendered a frank conversation about what we valued about participating and likewise what we found constraining. That led us to focus on a product—something that would help us to reflect on the value and process of our work together. We felt that the conversations were of definite value to us and wondered if they might also be of value to others. And if so, how might we capture and elaborate their interactive nature in print? So we decided to work toward publishing the conversations. In writing about what we did, we have sought to capture both the process of discussion—as set out in the structure of each chapter— and the outcomes of those discussions—as represented in these text versions.

Why Share These Conversations?
Capturing in printed form the ebb and flow of ideas that constituted the work of LTEC has been a major challenge. The first question we asked ourselves was, what is the possible value of these conversations to others in the field? Why share them? We would argue that there are three basic reasons: process, content, and professionalism.

First, making these conversations public may encourage others to similar undertakings. Putting the process in print opens it up to replication. The chapters in this book provide a series of maps showing how one group of ESOL teacher educators integrated a process of collaborative inquiry into their day-to-day jobs. Readers may decide to undertake a similar process of finding or writing a provocative text and inviting colleagues to have a collaborative conversation about it. Or readers may adopt only part of the process, perhaps the issues-based conversation. We feel that whatever encouragement the book may offer, those who engage in collaborative inquiry will find it beneficial.

Second, whether similar conversations are undertaken or not, the content as it is argued here seems to us so central to rigorous examination of

ESOL teacher education that it should not be overlooked. Putting the content in print gets these core issues on the table for discussion. In a sense, this content introduces the element of vulnerability that comes with inquiry. Readers may disagree that these issues are central, or they may question what individuals in these conversations say about the issues. But raising these major themes seems to us essential to opening up the work of ESOL teacher education to close, public examination.

Which leads to the third reason: professionalism. We believe that closely and reflectively examining how we educate ESOL teachers plays a critical part in professionalizing ESOL as a field. As in any field, ESOL teacher educators have areas of consensus and difference in what we think and do. Usually, however, we rehearse these issues in the third person of professional writing and scholarly journals. In a real sense, we are prisoners of that genre, which is one that leaves little—if any—room to write and talk together about how we do what we do and the tensions that are part of that work. These conversations depart from that norm. They raise messy issues, expose individual practitioners' thinking, and leave the issues unresolved, all of which is quite atypical of our professional genre. But we believe it can be quite useful. Unless and until we can speak rigorously about the core contradictions in what we ask ESOL teachers to know and do and how we ask them to learn it, our work will not rest on a firm foundation.

Book Format

The format of the LTEC meetings gradually became more stable and fixed. One member would generate a text (usually two to three pages in length) to distribute prior to the meeting, thus providing a set of focal issues. We rotated this responsibility to allow each group member to introduce issues he or she found compelling. Although in the early meetings a written response was the admission ticket, eventually the only requirement for attendance was having read and reflected on the text.

Each chapter of the book represents one LTEC meeting (in chronological order, although we have not included all the meetings). Each is divided into three parts. We begin with the preliminary text that was circulated prior to our meeting. We then provide an edited transcription of the discussion that the text engendered. This opens up not only the product—the issues discussed and points made by participants—but also the process. As will be apparent, discussions such as these are often messy, sometimes circular, and not always comfortable. Because we feel that these conditions were often the catalysts to our learning, we have attempted to capture and portray their essence.

One recurrent concern among us as teacher educators was that we were discussing teachers and teaching issues but not including the voices of classroom practitioners. The format of the book has allowed us to address that shortcoming. For each chapter, we have solicited a teacher respondent, someone who is knowledgeable and invested in the chapter's issues, and we have invited him or her to respond to the issues and viewpoints represented in the conversation. These responses constitute the third section of each chapter. At the end of each chapter, along with references, we have included a list of suggested further readings. The list combines works that LTEC members feel have provided a foundation for our thinking and our viewpoints on topics addressed in the chapter, and more recent pieces that may serve to push and extend the conversation. We hope you find them useful.

The chapters and topics addressed are as follows:

Collaborative Groups in Teacher Education

The text describes the experiences of a student who criticized the extensive use of collaborative groups in an ESOL methods course. In the conversation, LTEC members explore the sources of student resistance to group work; ways of helping students better understand the purposes and advantages of working in collaborative groups; the inevitable but necessary tensions that exist in such learning; and the impact of collaborative group work on the teacher educator's engagement, authority, and sense of control. The conversation takes stock of our different perspectives on the nature of knowledge, how it is learned, and the formats that can accommodate these perspectives. It ends with an appreciation for the complexity of what is often presented simply as a technique. The response is by a teacher who was a class member and whose experiences stimulated the original topic.

Can In-Service Professional Development Be Authentic?

The text reports on a survey study designed to discover which models of staff development in-service teachers prefer. The conversation focuses on differences between teacher education in a graduate classroom, where instruction can be carefully designed to reflect a learner-centered approach, and site-based professional development, where administrators often invite a consultant to provide brief workshops, with little follow-up to support teachers who experiment with new ideas or methods. We speculate on how teachers form preferences, share some site-based models that depart from the one-shot workshop approach, and discuss how we as professional development consultants might improve in-service education. The response is by a teacher who has received in-service training and who has strong feelings about professional development.

Controlling a Negotiated Syllabus
The text describes an LTEC member's attempts to have students participate in planning a methodology course by helping to construct the course syllabus. The conversation discusses the advantages and disadvantages of using this kind of process syllabus, the teacher's role in negotiating class content and procedures, and issues of authority and control. As always in our conversations, many of the issues we raise have no simple answers: What mixed messages do we send if we are not willing to negotiate everything in the syllabus? How might students benefit from resisting the process? How do differences between the informal negotiation that occurs when problems arise and a formal mechanism for negotiation affect the process? The response is by a teacher learner who was "negotiated" (his term) in a class taught by the writer of the text.

The Nature of Linguistics in a Language Teacher Education Program
The text is an excerpt from a published article by an LTEC member on the role of linguistics in language teacher education. In it, she points out that all language teacher education programs require students to study linguistics and asks what prospective language teachers should be expected to take away from these courses. The conversation centers on the aspects of linguistic study that could enable students to construct their own understanding of the language they have chosen to teach. A related issue is whether or not there exist decontextualized linguistic facts that our students should be expected to learn. The response is by an elementary school ESL teacher who describes how she uses grammatical knowledge in her classroom.

Examining Language Teachers' Teaching Knowledge

The text is an excerpt from a conference presentation given by two LTEC members, which was a dialogue about what a language teacher's teaching knowledge is and how we, as teacher educators, can teach it. The conversation addresses the questions: What is teaching knowledge for a language teacher? What is the relationship between teaching knowledge and the array of courses, such as linguistics, methodology, and second language acquisition, generally found in a program for language teachers? How can we teach this teaching knowledge? If teaching knowledge is context-based, is the university context irrelevant? The discussion also touches on the difficult issue of defining good teaching. The response is by a teacher who was trained in a program that focused on teaching knowledge.

The Role of Research in Language Teacher Education

The text raises broad theoretical and pedagogical questions about the role of research in language teacher education, disciplinary boundaries of research, and appropriate perspectives and methodologies for exploring classroom environments. It then provides one member's reflections on her own research in light of these issues. In the conversation, LTEC members present their own histories and stories about beginning to engage in research and view themselves as researchers. We explore and debate definitions of research, what value we feel it has, and for whom. We discuss the divide between researcher and practitioner: why we feel it exists, what we feel our role is, and the paradox of mentoring and evaluating while wanting equal status with those we mentor and evaluate. We reflect on our values and beliefs, and our goals for engaging in academics. The response is by an elementary school teacher who has engaged in collaborative classroom-based research with a member of the LTEC group.

The book's conclusion, "Closely Examined Work: An Epilogue to the LTEC Conversation," situates the group's work in current research and practice in language teaching and learning. It connects themes and issues from the conversations to current issues in language teaching, language teacher education, and the continuing professional development of language teachers and language teacher educators.

REFERENCES

Allwright, D. (2003). Exploratory practice: Rethinking practitioner research in language teaching. *Language Teaching Research, 7,* 113–142.

Appel, J. (1995). *Diary of a language teacher.* London: Heinemann.

Bailey. F. (1996). The role of collaborative dialogue in teacher education. In D. Freeman & J. C. Richards (Eds.), *Teacher learning in language teaching* (pp. 260–280). Cambridge, England: Cambridge University Press.

Ballenger, C. (1999). *Teaching other people's children: Literacy and learning in a bilingual classroom.* New York: Teachers College Press.

Britzman, D. (1991). *Practice makes practice: A critical study of learning to teach.* Albany: State University of New York Press.

Clair, N. (1998). Teacher study groups: Persistent problems in a promising approach. *TESOL Quarterly, 32,* 465–492.

Edge, J. (2002). *Continuing cooperative professional development.* Ann Arbor: University of Michigan Press.

Florio-Ruane, S. (2001). *Teacher education and the cultural imagination.* Mahwah, NJ: Lawrence Erlbaum.

Freedman, S. W., Simons, E. R., Kalnin, J. S., & Casareno, A. (1999). *Inside city schools: Investigating literacy in multicultural classrooms.* New York: Teachers College Press.

Freeman, D., & Johnson, K. E. (1998). Reconceptualizing the knowledge-base of language teacher education. *TESOL Quarterly, 32,* 397–417.

Freeman, D., & Richards, J. C. (1996). *Teacher learning in language teaching.* New York: Cambridge University Press.

Grossman, P., Wineburg, S., & Woolworth, S. (2001). Toward a theory of teacher community. *Teachers College Record, 103,* 942–1012.

Hawkins, M. (2000). The reassertion of traditional authority in a constructivist pedagogy. *Teaching Education, 11,* 279–296.

Hollingsworth, S. (1994). *Teacher research and urban literacy education: Lessons and conversations in a feminist key.* New York: Teachers College Press.

Johnson, K. E. (1999). *Understanding language teaching: Reasoning in action.* Boston: Heinle & Heinle.

Macgillivray, L. (1997). Do what I say, not what I do: An instructor rethinks her own teaching and research. *Curriculum Inquiry, 27,* 469–488.

Ramanathan, V. (2002). *The politics of TESOL education: Writing, knowledge, critical pedagogy.* New York: Routledge Falmer.

Richards, J. C., & Lockhart, C. (1994). *Reflective teaching in second language classrooms.* New York: Cambridge University Press.

Richards, J. C., & Nunan, D. (1990). *Second language teacher education.* New York: Cambridge University Press.

Samuel, M. (1998). Changing lives in changing times: Preservice teacher education in post-apartheid South Africa. *TESOL Quarterly, 32*, 576–583.

Souza Lima, E. (1998). Teachers as learners: The dialectics of improving pedagogical practice in Brazil. In G. L. Anderson & M. Montero-Sieburth (Eds.), *Educational qualitative research in Latin America: The struggle for a new paradigm* (pp. 141–160). New York: Garland.

Stevick, E. (1980). *Teaching languages: A way and ways.* Rowley, MA: Newbury House.

Teacher Knowledge Project. (2003). *The Teacher Knowledge Project: Making teacher inquiry an integral part of professional development.* Retrieved December 26, 2003, from http://www.sit.edu /tkp

Willett, J., & Miller, S. (2004). Transforming the discourses of teaching and learning: Rippling waters and shifting sands. In M. Hawkins (Ed.), *Language learning and teacher education: A sociocultural approach.* Clevedon, England: Multilingual Matters.

Yates, R., & Muchisky, D. (2003). On reconceptualizing teacher education. *TESOL Quarterly, 37*, 135–146.

Zeichner, K. (1999). The new scholarship in teacher education. *Educational Researcher, 28*(2), 4–15.

Zeichner, K., & Liston, D. (1996). *Reflective teaching: An introduction.* Mahwah, NJ: Lawrence Erlbaum.

1

Collaborative Groups in Teacher Education

TEXT

Francis Bailey and Jerri Willett

> *The old transmission model part of me wishes there had been more nuts-and-bolts material from you . . . um . . . perhaps* lectures *(heavens do I admit this!? Old modes die hard!). I realize this contradicts so much of what you tried to convey.*
>
>

Methods course evaluation, Tom Nicoletti

The use of small learning groups in teacher education is widespread. Small groups enable students to explore topics in much greater depth than might be possible in larger, teacher-centered educational forums. Working in these groups has a special payoff in teacher education because it forces students to confront a variety of core educational issues around the roles of teachers and students in learning. However, we also realize that there is nothing magical about putting students into groups, nothing that guarantees a positive learning experience. We would like to draw on our collaborative research in a second language methods course to explore a set of tensions that lie at the heart of this educational practice.

In the epigraph, Tom questions his experience with small-group learning. Tom was a member of a methods course for second language teachers at the University of Massachusetts–Amherst. This course was designed around small groups of students researching topics in second language learning and then teaching their classmates about their topics.

Tom's critique centers on his desire for what he has elsewhere called "hard information"; that is, knowledge from experts in the field such as the instructor and authors of texts. As his comment suggests, he would have preferred that the instructor deliver this knowledge in the form of lectures. Clearly, he recognizes that his desire for a more traditional educational experience is at odds with the philosophy of the course.

The following are two core tensions that we have identified with small-group learning in teacher education.

(a) Small-group learning positions students in new roles, which can cause anxiety, fear, and resistance. But it also forces them to confront a variety of core issues concerning the nature of learning and teaching.

Small-group learning is often quite stressful. Asking equal status peers to work collaboratively on a task is a challenging assignment. Working out the group dynamics often takes a lot of time and energy for group members, and groups usually struggle with this process. Anyone who has worked with this form of education has almost certainly encountered groups in which anger, frustration, and tears were part of the not-so-hidden curriculum. On the other hand, we have observed that those groups often enable students to explore their own assumptions about the nature of teacher authority and student responsibility, the role of social interaction in learning, and a host of related issues. The experience of working in groups can force students to confront their own deep-seated expectations about learning and teaching.

We have identified this tension as central to the experience of small-group learning because the powerful emotions that the experience can unearth arise at the juncture between how students expect to be educated and how working in a group challenges those basic assumptions. Although students may be more comfortable with an educational experience that provides "nuts-and-bolts material" delivered by the instructor, small-group learning can make explicit the students' tacit conceptions of education. Inherent in that process are students' emotional responses to being asked to confront their assumptions, push beyond them, and learn in fundamentally new ways.

(b) Small-group learning requires students to use one another as resources and to struggle communally to make sense of course content, but it can also deprive them of an instructor who can scaffold their efforts. Collaborative learning minimizes a teacher's opportunity to interact directly with students around course content. Hence, teachers may not be able to scaffold students in their encounters with course materials. Our research shows that this aspect of collaborative learning had at least two important consequences.

Small-group learning forced students to rely on themselves. They did not have access to outside experts so they had to think through issues themselves and rely on other group members as resources. Although this type of educational design fostered self-reliance, it tended at times to frustrate students who felt it impeded progress toward a firm understanding of the course content. The conversations were all too often diffuse and without a tight enough focus to enable the group to plumb a subject's depths. Some groups also had difficulty in gaining a deep understanding of their core textbook. They were never able to use (as a group) the information that the text provided to gain insight into their topic.

Both of these difficulties result directly from the absence of a teacher who would focus the group discussion on an idea or set of ideas and who would scaffold students' understanding of a key text.

Our research showed that group members genuinely pooled their knowledge. They helped each other figure out what the text was about, based on their own knowledge of the subject matter and their life experiences with language teaching and learning. As Tom's comment shows, however, some group members felt the need for the authoritative voice of an expert who could help them understand the core ideas in their readings and tasks. Moreover, the students' struggle with these core ideas engendered anxiety in the teacher. Even though the teacher could respond to the groups' products (presentations and papers in this case), she had an ever present, uneasy feeling that the students "wouldn't get it" without more direct instruction.

Teacher educators do not seek to resolve these tensions because we believe that they enable learning. Paradoxically, however, these same tensions can cause group work to fail. How can we manage and exploit these tensions to increase student learning but lower the affective filter (of both students and teacher)?

DESCRIPTION OF THE COURSE

Jerri Willett

The ESL methods and materials course was designed to help students explore whole language approaches and methods for teaching ESL. We aimed to design a course that (a) centered on learners' experiences and understandings while apprenticing them to the discourse of ESL teaching; (b) engaged them in authentic and interactive tasks on which they worked collaboratively; (c) supported their participation and learning in these tasks; and (d) encouraged them to reflect on their participation and learning throughout the course. The students were a heterogeneous group that included experienced teachers of children, adolescents, and adults; international students; newcomers to the field of ESL; and doctoral students. Although the course was designed around a particular perspective of teaching ESL, we expected the diversity of the group to encourage critical dialogue about the methods and perspectives presented in the course.

The course was structured in the following way: (a) For the first half of each class, approximately 70 minutes, the professor presented the whole language principles that she wanted the students to explore. (b) For the second half of each class, students met in their assigned small groups to explore a particular method and to prepare an interactive presentation for the full class. (c) Near the end of the semester, the small groups presented their methods to the full class in a way that embodied the whole language principles and led a critical discussion with the class about the method. These methods included problem posing, simulation and role playing, reading and writing for those with limited literacy skills, content-based instruction, peer response groups in writing workshop, and literature-based instruction.

In addition to the principles that oriented the course, the course supported small-group work in a variety of ways. First, each group had a facilitator who helped members reflect on their group's processes. Facilitators were experienced teachers or doctoral students who explored collaborative learning by studying their own groups and presenting their understandings to the full class. Second, the members of each group were given reading materials to help them explore their topics. (Tom's group did not like the book they were assigned, however, and they rejected it.) Third, each group had sufficiently diverse resources, experiences, talents, and background knowledge among its members to ensure that they could complete their task. Fourth, the course included a variety of practices that encouraged and supported critical reflection, including dialogue journals between facilitators and their group members, written peer responses to the presentations, the professor's written responses for the class about issues that arose during each presentation, and the professor's feedback on individual projects in which students developed a lesson or unit using one or more of the approaches presented in class.

CONVERSATION

FRANCIS: The person we focused on in our text, Tom, was a student in one of the small groups, and he was very invested in this process. He really struggled with attempting to learn in this format. I thought he'd be an interesting one to discuss because he's one of our "good" students. Tom's statement crystallizes a couple of ideas that are operating in small groups, and some of the tensions that we've laid out here. I think part of his resistance came from his desire to hear the voice of the instructor. He needed reassurance that what he was doing was acceptable as part of the discourse of the field that he was trying to enter. He did see the balance between knowledge transmitted by a teacher and knowledge constructed by students. He was really invested in this process. He did try to make sense of this, but at the end of the semester, he wasn't convinced.

DIANE: The more you try to come to grips with what the central issue is here, the more elusive it becomes. It seems to me there are three sets of issues. One is the unclear expectations, students wondering, "What am I going to be graded on?" Students have to be persuaded by the value of the process, but at least that's something you can deal with. The second thing is that we need to appreciate what it means to ask people to work in small groups and not just assume that it means doing the same thing they would be doing individually but doing it together. I've made this mistake before, not preparing people adequately or not helping them to cope with some of the group dynamics issues that often arise. The third thing has to do with an appeal to authority and students worrying about who has the answers here, and it seems to me that was maybe the focal issue, although they are all intertwined.

Unclear Expectations

MAGGIE: As far as expectations go, you've got the issue of whether students are being graded on how they work in a group. They think, "If the group process and how we work it out is part of my grade, what does that mean? Does it mean if I smile and I'm nice to everybody I get an A? Or does it mean that if I think the group is going in the wrong direction and I try to go somewhere else I'm disruptive?"

DIANE: From my experience getting the kind of reaction that Tom gave, it comes from a place of fear. So I'm trying to understand the process. What is the source of the threat here? One possible source is not understanding the content; another is failing to deliver it in a process way that honors the content. One way to get at Tom's concern is to ask, "How could a student fail at this task?"

FRANCIS: The way they're positioned in this class makes a lot of people uncomfortable. Their group is the only group that's going to present their particular topic, so the pressure's on them. They came into the class as students, but they're being positioned as experts— and as teachers—in relation to their peers.

ELLEN: Jerri, you were saying there is an agenda, in terms of the principles and what it is you hope the students will learn. I would think that as a student in that class, I would be worried during the entire class about "getting it," finding out what you want to hear and telling it to you. Do you feel that tension from the students?

JERRI: I don't think it's a major one. People start out thinking that way, and wondering, "Will I be able to do it?" and "What does she want?" But in the process of actually trying to figure it out, they get so involved that they forget about their grades. I never get the question, "What grade am I getting?"

MAGGIE: I think it has to do with the fact that the structure sets up a whole different environment. A shift takes place somewhere within the first month. They begin to look at each other as a learning community that shares, and they come to look at the instructor differently, not quite as one of them, but not in the traditional way. When it works well, people do get empowered. They do find that they have a voice, that their perspective is valued.

JERRI: One of the things I'm concerned about is the anxiety about the process. It's real for a lot of people in the beginning, although as they come to see the process, the anxiety lessens. Students see the purpose and see how it works. Some of them are totally fascinated by it. Others say, "Well, yes, that's fine, but not for me." But by the end, most people begin to understand what's going on. The issue I've been grappling with is that, theoretically, you need to go through that cognitive dissonance in order to begin understanding some of these issues. The tension is in how you prevent unnecessary anxiety. Do we *have* to make students go through torture to learn some of these concepts? Is there a way to support the process a little bit more so people don't feel lost? Or is this something they just have to go through?

SUZANNE: One question I have is whether, if you try to forestall some of these tensions, you change the whole process and therefore change the learning that occurs through the process. For example, what happens if you talk about it beforehand, and let students know what they're in for so they'll be better able to deal with it?

MAGGIE: That's an interesting question because it doesn't really work well to lay it all out beforehand. Later, when they're experiencing something, they don't remember that they've been told. It needs to be said at exactly the moment that they need it said. No matter how much you explain beforehand, it's too much because they don't have anything to relate it to. Then when they get there and they need to understand it, they've forgotten everything you said before. It's very frustrating.

JERRI: I know. Students would ask, "Why didn't you tell us?" But I did. My first response was to make the process more and more explicit, so the descriptions of what we were doing got longer and longer. But as I became more explicit, their efforts to figure out what I wanted increased rather than lessened. So the idea of explicit framing, that you can just tell people, isn't the answer by itself.

MAGGIE: And you've got another tension. As you become more explicit and you frame it more, you're narrowing what they do and directing it. That goes against the initial concept of letting them explore and choose directions.

JERRI: One thing that I haven't done is to assign roles. The only role that I stipulate has been the facilitator role. In my last class we were reading Elizabeth Cohen's book [Cohen, 1994], in which she talks about the need for roles in the group. One of the groups decided that their group was not going well because they didn't assign roles, so they started doing this. They felt it helped their group process a lot. So in their presentation they emphasized the need for roles, and talked about how some of the problems that groups were having could be taken care of by assigning roles and taking more responsibility for the process.

SUZANNE: I want to relate that to the idea of being explicit. If you told them that it would be a good idea for the groups to develop roles and to appoint people to the roles, then they would get back into this idea of, "What is it she wants us to do, and how are we supposed to do it?"

JERRI: Right. The experience was powerful because they came to this conclusion themselves.

SUZANNE: But do they always have to come to it themselves? If they do, then you can't get rid of the tension.

Group Dynamics

FRANCIS: From a teacher educator's point of view, it's interesting that the same issues that arise here also arise in ESL classes. If you try to implement cooperative learning in a high school class, for example, you're going to have personality conflicts and people who don't believe in this form of learning. With this format, we have a chance to model for our teachers, in the particular context of this teacher education class, how we deal with these issues. We're saying, "Yes, we're going to deal with real problems here," and then we try to work them out. There are going to be different levels of success, but we can at least engage with issues that are similar to the ones our students are going to be dealing with in their own classes.

MAGGIE: I was thinking of something when we were talking about whether it has to be uncomfortable, whether there has to be this sort of disequilibrium. I think *cognitive dissonance* is the term Jerri used. If these students, particularly the native English speaking students, feel uncomfortable working within this format in a graduate course, think what their students feel. These are ESL teachers, their students are nonnative English speaking, they don't have the language, they don't have the culture, they don't even necessarily know the culture of schooling. It's not a bad thing to point out that if they're feeling like they're in a new format, with new expectations and new sorts of roles, what must their students feel?

JERRI: Right. It's probably also important to talk about what you're feeling as the teacher as well because this is not comfortable. Having your whole class come in and say "What is this all about?" is very emotional. And because it's emotional, it's also extremely engaging.

23

You don't become disengaged in your teaching because you are emotionally involved with what your students are doing and with what's going to happen. You don't have total control over it; it's a dialogue.

MAGGIE: And it's not formulaic, so it's not like when you've done it once, you have it down. It changes with the people and with the dynamics.

JERRI: Right, it changes. So in every class you learn something that you can use the next time. One of the nice things about teacher education is that no matter what happens, it's relevant because you're in a classroom. If you think of it in that way, whatever happens in the classroom can become the content of the class. This shifts it completely away from personality conflicts or whatever problems you're having to something broader and more principled.

FRANCIS: I've been thinking about the issue of students' emotions. In a classroom lecture format there is frustration among students, but it's not public frustration. People are usually very passive in class, and then they go home and try to write their papers. And they pull out their hair, or throw the computer out the window. But it's private frustration. In this model, because you have to work in a group, you're making a lot of the emotional component public.

JERRI: These feelings and anxieties are there anyway. One of the things that happens in this kind of organization is that you know about their concerns and therefore you can deal with them, whereas in a teacher-fronted transmission classroom, you don't know about them. It's not that they're not there.

Appeal to Authority

DIANE: I mentioned earlier that there might be three reasons for Tom's response: unclear expectations, group dynamics, and issues around authority. I'd like to move on to the appeal to authority issue, if we could.

FRANCIS: One of the authority issues that's interesting to me is that, in some ways, I feel like it's illusory that we're giving authority to students. What I saw in my research was a lot of Jerri's voice coming out through other people's mouths. Ventriloquism was really common.

MAGGIE: But I don't look at it as giving the students the authority. Maybe Tom felt like Jerri wasn't taking the authority, but I don't see it as giving students authority that they wouldn't otherwise have. My underlying rationale is that people make meaning by exploring and negotiating ideas in social interaction, so it's not that I'm abdicating my authority. It's that I am giving them the structure within which to explore ideas and make meaning of them for themselves and with each other. If I just explain these ideas and meanings to them, I don't think they get as much out of it. But I'm not fooling myself into thinking that I don't care if they get out of it what I want them to.

FRANCIS: Let me give you a very specific example of students' authority. In this class, they have the right to reject the textbook. In most classrooms, you don't have this right. You don't have to read it—you can kind of fudge it—but basically you have to deal with that text because the teacher's going to hold you accountable. The teacher's going to continue working with that text. Exams and papers should somehow reflect something that came out of that text, and you're supposed to know that knowledge. But in Tom's group, they didn't have to do that. They tried to make sense of it, but they really couldn't, so they just said, "We're going to bag it and use other materials." It seems to me that they did have some authority.

DIANE: What if we take Tom's comment at face value? What he says is, "I need hard information." We could say he had access to a text and other materials, and he did, but that clearly was not enough. This is the kind of thing I wrestle with, students saying, "We want to hear it from *you*, Diane." If we are seeking to empower students about their own learning, and to learn from one another, it might be that we accomplish this by responding to their requests for information, not by withholding it. It seems to me that if somebody asks me for information and I respond, I may be giving in to them, but I'm also respecting the student's appeal and empowering them by obliging. It's never a black and white issue; you have to make that judgment every single time.

ELLEN: I think there can be a frustration on the part of students because they feel that they're with someone who *is* an expert, so they feel that the professor is being arrogant by saying, "I know the answer but I won't give it to you, you have to find it out for yourself." Even if it's not taken as arrogant, it's still a frustration. It's as if an ESL teacher were to say, "You have to translate this but you can't look in a dictionary. You have to figure out every word from context."

MAGGIE: It's very comfortable for students to think that there are experts out there who have the answers, that they can tell you how to teach well. Then you can walk into a classroom, do exactly what they say, and be a good teacher.

SUZANNE: I think part of the problem is Tom's lack of any kind of experience in finding answers for himself. People have been exposed to so much transmission teaching that turning them around is a major undertaking. I think what we're seeing in Tom is just a lack of enough experience to show him that he really can do it himself.

MAGGIE: But as soon as he says, "I can't come to it myself," he's assuming there's an "it" to come to. That goes back to the assumption that there's a right way, that there *are* answers out there. But I don't see teaching that way. Teaching is not saying, "There are pieces of information that I have, and if I tell them to you and you can tell them back to me, you will be a well-educated person." Therefore, in a system where you are told, "It's in this text, it's in this teacher, and when you memorize and can spit back what they say, you've got it," you're still looking for "it."

FRANCIS: Tom talked about his desire for "hard information." If you think about the word *hard*, what he wants is something that's stable.

He has an orientation toward knowledge that suggests that it's outside of him, it's stable, it's going to be there for him, and there are ways to get access to it. It's a foundation. But another way of looking at it is that knowledge is contingent, we're always creating it. It's not outside people, it's between people. I think that's the tension Tom is reflecting. He understood the course process and appreciated it, but still he needed to know, "Where are the nuggets of knowledge that I can hold on to?"

DIANE: Because his assumption is that there are these "nuggets of knowledge." There's a different sense of what knowledge is. So you still have the same questions: How do you frame the difference? Do you tell them what it is? Do they have to experience it? You still have to deal with the same issues, the group dynamics, the emotional issues, all of that. I do that, but I still keep getting, "We want to hear it from you."

Learning to Teach

FRANCIS: I think we have to abandon this idea that teachers can learn to teach from our courses. They're not going to get skills from sitting in our classes. They're going to encounter certain kinds of questions current in the field. They can learn about language analysis; they can learn about ideas that are floating around out there. They can test things out on themselves, but ultimately they're not going to learn to teach in our classrooms. And there's nothing we can do about that.

JERRI: But they have been learning to teach all along, through 15 years of transmission. I hear people say, "Well, they don't know anything yet, so how can they do it?" Of course they know something; they know a whole lot, and that's the problem. We're showing them alternatives so they have something else to draw on when they begin teaching. What you put together is an accumulation of your experiences, both with yourself as a learner and with your students in the classroom, and you're drawing on both of them. You will throw out some of the things from your experience as being irrelevant in this other setting, and some of them you'll draw on heavily. I don't think it's always easy to predict where knowledge of teaching comes from. Part of what we're trying to do is problematize the framework that students bring with them to our classrooms.

MAGGIE: I would also claim that teaching isn't something that they're going to learn to do anywhere. It's an ongoing process of discovery that you refine as you do it. Part of our job is to give our students whatever they need to go into their classrooms and learn how to look reflectively at their own teaching. It's an ongoing process once they've left our classrooms, no matter what they learned there. We couldn't do it in a semester, or a year, or 2 years, even if there was an "it" to be done.

DIANE: So that's it. You can't do it, even if it could be done. There's no "it" to be done.

RESPONSE

Tom Nicoletti

I want to thank all of you for sharing your transcript with me. It is very interesting reading. For someone who first experienced small-group learning in Jerri's series of courses, it is very enlightening to listen to a group of teacher educators discuss this approach. I must admit that having my words and experience serve as a vehicle of the discussion causes a certain amount of embarrassment. I was quite new to the program at that time. But if my experience can provide a useful example of how some students respond to small-group learning, then I'm happy for that.

Thanks also for inviting me to offer an update and reactions to the discussion. I should begin by saying that during my program in the School of Education I quickly grew to appreciate the value of the small-group projects that Jerri assigned. You could say that I am now a believer in that process. I think the learning that goes on in that kind of experientially based approach is difficult, if not impossible, to achieve with other formats. The process may not always be especially comfortable, but by being so engaged and invested in it, learners come to own their work in a way that does not happen with other approaches. I think it is a wonderfully effective way to integrate theory and practice. These experiences in group work taught me to value my classmates and the kinds of contributions that students themselves can make, based on their own experience and knowledge. Although I think mini-lectures have their value in some situations, lectures are a problematic mode of instruction and communication. I think there are other, more creative, more involving ways to teach.

I still feel quite new to teaching, and in group work I still have to confront personal issues of expertise and authority. But I am learning that the main issue is about process and context, not the existence of some body of decontextualized hard facts. In another class, a professor said something that has stayed with me, and which I think relates to the "it" that Maggie mentions. He was discussing publishing in education, and he asked us how we regarded new articles and books in the field. Did we view them as advances in our knowledge, as though they were bricks being added to the edifice of Education? I was just about to nod in assent when he said, "No, that's not it. They are all just part of a 'conversation' about how we think things work." I find this a meaningful way to express the concept that all our ideas, our knowledge, occur within a context, and we are just conversing about how, at this time, we perceive their nature. It sounds so elementary, and on a larger scale it's something that I've intuitively understood and agreed with for a long time. Perhaps when people are new to a field of endeavor, what they are really asking when they look to authorities for the answers and the knowledge is, "How do I become part of this conversation? What do I need to participate?" What I now see as important is not some disconnected collection of facts but the frame of reference for a body of knowledge. And I think that small-group learning can offer students an effective means for exploring this. I agree with your group that explicit framing at the beginning of a project is not particularly helpful; I think discussion becomes much more meaningful after students have grappled with the issues for a while. Also, at the end of the course, students can discuss the framework as they reflect on the process they have engaged in.

With regard to stress and anxiety, I agree with the group that these feelings are inherent in the process. For me, grading was never an issue. I learned quickly that Jerri respected each learner's background and "starting place" and the progress that each person was able to make. So I never worried about my grade. Most of my stress arose from questions to myself: "Okay, I don't have much experience with this subject and these issues, how can I contribute to the group's success?" (expressed not in a despairing way, but rather in a practical and matter-of-fact sense), and "How is our group going to work together on this to produce something that reflects our work exploring the material and the issues and is useful for our classmates?" In our classes, I remember that we talked about another source of tension, a built-in one: the tension between students' desire to delve into theory and fully explore the issues and the need to produce something presentable by the end of the semester. I remember very well how our group struggled to examine in depth, "What is content?" Before we could agree that we had finished with this issue, we felt pressure to assemble a presentation that we hoped would convey something of what we had learned.

I agree with Francis and others in your discussion group that students will encounter these issues in their practice as teachers. Gaining experience in dealing with them will inform our work as professionals. To be sure, at times I wished the whole process could be less stressful, but I think that increasing student (and teacher) comfort could mean losing some of the students' initiative and learning. These courses are so valuable and rewarding because they require a high degree of engagement, even if students sometimes feel uncomfortable. Reading the transcript and Francis and Jerri's introduction makes me appreciate the fact that this teaching approach can also create stress for the instructor.

In your discussion you referred to students' cognitive dissonance, and Jerri asked, "Do we *have* to make students go through torture to learn some of these concepts? Is there a way to support that process a little bit more so people don't feel lost? Or is this something they just have to go through?" To all of these questions I would answer, "Yes." I think a certain amount of "torture," of "getting through," is necessary and helpful, but I also think that scaffolding can be helpful, especially for people with less teaching experience or who come from different cultural and linguistic backgrounds.

In another class, Jerri had us engage in a jigsaw activity whereby everyone learned what the other groups were doing, how they were progressing, and so forth. Our group, and members from other groups that I talked with, found this activity extremely useful. It enabled us to compare notes with each other and learn from other groups' experiences. I think that another such activity later in the process would have been valuable as well. This is one kind of activity that can help ease some of the students' tension without sacrificing their initiative. It enables groups to confer with each other, and with the instructor at intermediate points in the process and allows them to make useful adjustments. I think I will use this activity in my own teaching.

I feel extremely fortunate to have been introduced to this teaching approach in these classes. Even though I am hoping to teach in East Asia, where students may be accustomed to lectures and unfamiliar or uncomfortable with other forms of teaching, I look forward to adapting small-group learning for my own classes. It should be an interesting challenge.

ACKNOWLEDGMENTS

This chapter contains text, conversation, and response from F. Bailey, M. Hawkins, S. Irujo, D. Larsen-Freeman, E. Rintell, and J. Willett, "Language Teacher Educators' Collaborative Conversations," *TESOL Quarterly, 32*, pp. 536–546.

REFERENCES

Cohen, E. G. (1994). *Designing group work: Strategies for the heterogeneous classroom.* New York: Teachers College Press.

PROMOTING FURTHER CONVERSATIONS

Bailey, F. (1996). The role of collaborative dialogue in teacher education. In D. Freeman & J. Richards (Eds.), *Teacher learning in language teaching* (pp. 260–280). Cambridge, England: Cambridge University Press.

Cohen, E. G. (1994). *Designing group work: Strategies for the heterogeneous classroom.* New York: Teachers College Press.

Comeaux, M. (1991). But is it "teaching"? The use of collaborative learning in teacher education. In R. Tabachnich & K. Zeichner (Eds.), *Issues and practices in inquiry-oriented teacher education* (pp. 151–165). London: Falmer.

Miller, J. (1990). *Creating spaces and finding voices.* Albany: State University of New York Press.

Slavin, R. E. (1995). *Cooperative learning: Theory, research, and practice.* Boston: Allyn & Bacon.

2

Can In-Service Professional Development Be Authentic?

TEXT

Ellen Rintell

I have been grappling with how to make training for teachers most effective and authentic. As a college professor, I am frequently invited as a consultant to do in-service staff development. In this role, I seem to fall back into presenting what are euphemistically called *workshops*, but what are often lectures. If an administrator feels that teachers working with language minority students need to know more about language acquisition and asks me to give a 90-minute workshop, it is hard to avoid the lecture format. Even when I can avoid it, it is still a 90-minute experience. Follow-up will depend on the energy and will of teachers inspired enough to experiment in their classrooms or to begin reading and researching.

Now that teachers have to renew their certification every 5 years by accruing points given largely for attending such professional development workshops,[1] any attempt to reform staff development must engage them in

---

[1] At the time of this conversation, Massachusetts had just passed legislation eliminating lifetime teacher certification and requiring teachers to renew their certification every 5 years by acquiring a certain number of professional development points.

the reform process. Therefore, I decided to ask teachers what they thought about their professional development experiences and what professional development models they found most useful. I organized a panel at the state bilingual education conference to discuss this issue with bilingual and ESL teachers, and I presented the graduate students in my ESL methods course (all practicing teachers) with the same questions.

During the conference presentation, we introduced various models of professional development and asked participants to talk to one another about a set of written questions, then we opened the floor for discussion.

When we asked, "What questions do you think we should be asking about staff development?," respondents raised the following questions:

- How can teachers request professional development and not feel they are admitting ignorance or incompetence?
- How do we validate what teachers are already doing?
- How do we help teachers become researchers?
- How do we provide support for teachers' experiments?
- How do we help staff identify their needs?
- How do we reach "resistant" teachers who need development?

When we asked, "Which [professional development] experiences have been most positive for you, and why?," we received the following responses:

- Technology, because it gave me experience on the computer.
- I like classes where I can come away with actual lessons or methods to use with my students.
- I find presentations given by teachers the most relevant because the presenters have classroom experience.
- Credit courses were more positive because I felt I was working toward something.
- Workshops that allowed sharing of ideas among teachers on what has worked well in the classroom.

When we asked, "What kind of professional development do you believe is most useful for you as a teacher? What motivates you to learn more, implement a new practice in the classroom, and leads to student success?," we received the following responses:

- Anything that has worked in someone else's classroom.
- Hands-on practice and sharing with colleagues.
- Technology workshops.

- Small group setting with maximum self-reliance for setting goals, procedures, evaluation, etc.
- Learning strategies.
- Ideas that I can use immediately in my classroom.
- You tell me!
- I'd like time to visit teachers in action, but I'd be reluctant to open my classroom to streams of visitors.
- Things that I am allowed to choose.

These examples reflect the variety of answers we received to our questions. Most frequently, respondents answered with a topic they were interested in, such as learning strategies or technology. Some respondents wanted lessons, texts, or activities, "anything I can really use in my classroom." Some responded with an honest "you tell me" or did not respond at all. And some respondents commented on how professional development is presented to teachers and about the extent to which teachers themselves have a voice in planning and implementing professional development experiences.

These responses illustrate what teachers want and what they need, and why some teachers resist. To name a topic in this context is appropriate and understandable. After all, if teachers hear and read that society will increasingly depend on technology, that technology will transform education, and that therefore schoolchildren will have to become computer literate, then they might admit that they need technology skills and want to acquire them. Teachers do not lose face by admitting that they know little about an area that perhaps did not even exist when they received their own formal education. The same applies to topics such as violence prevention, or how to use the new mathematics series adopted by the community, both of which appeared in the data.

Naming a topic also suggests that teachers are willing to learn something easily identified as new to everyone, which does not force them to critically examine their own teaching. This type of response recalls one of our original questions: "How can teachers request professional development and not feel they are admitting ignorance or incompetence?" The survey and discussion allowed teachers to define *useful* or *effective*, but I think this question assumes that for an experience to influence teachers' professional growth, they must see it as in some way challenging what they know or what they believe to be best practice (Lange & Burroughs-Lange, 1994). Similarly, when teachers ask for "something I can use in my classroom," they are not only being practical but are also commenting on their many experiences with system-mandated in-service lectures or courses, which they were required to attend but which they found irrelevant.

The teacher who responded that she wanted to see other teachers in action raises two important issues: the need to learn by observing other successful teachers, and how rarely public school structures allow that kind of observation. At the same time, this teacher's reluctance to be observed once again suggests the fear of being judged, the fear that asking for professional development will make one appear incompetent.

The teacher who responded "small group setting with maximum self-reliance for setting goals, procedures, evaluation, etc." comes closest to my own view of ideal professional development. If, as teacher educators, we are promoting authentic instruction, then we must find ways to create contexts for authentic professional development. Professional development experiences are most meaningful when teachers themselves plan and implement them.

I had hoped that this project would provide insight about the settings in which teachers feel they learn best, but I think that a number of other issues must be resolved before we can address the details of any particular learning experience. These issues arise from the school systems' administrative structures, which still treat professional development as something to be required of teachers. In many cases, administrators apply it as something done to teachers rather than collaboratively with them. For authentic professional development to occur, school systems must be restructured to involve teachers from the earliest stages in its planning and implementation.

CONVERSATION

ELLEN: In my teaching, I have been involved with teacher education that's more in-service development than that which normally takes place within a graduate school classroom. My students are all practicing teachers, and they have been a source of reflection for me around what I've thought of as resistance—resistance to the notion that one can be reflective about teaching, that a teacher would want to make adjustments or grow. I wanted to see what would happen if I asked teachers what they thought they wanted. I optimistically expected that by asking these kinds of questions, the answers would represent teachers reflecting on how they learn best, their own knowledge about the way in which they would like to learn. I was surprised that I got such a variety of answers. For example, I got a lot of answers about what topic they wanted professional development about, rather than answers such as "I learn best in small groups," or "I learn best when I get to choose what the topic is." I even expected some of the issues that came from our discussion of Francis and Jerri's paper [see chapter 1], issues of whether they want to hear knowledge from an "expert," as compared to something more experiential. I was interested in what people felt about those things, and I do think it's possible to get at that. Perhaps the way I asked the questions didn't lead to that.

Setting Agendas

SUZANNE: I think they're responding based entirely on what they have experienced since they became teachers. They were given a teaching certificate that says, "You're a teacher, you know what you're doing, you can now go out and do it for the rest of your life." Most of them were not trained in being reflective, and in-service has always been something that's been done to them.

FRANCIS: The system doesn't have to be top-down. A research project could fit well within that, a research project that the teacher conceived of and conducted.

SUZANNE: If the culture of the school is such that teachers have never been encouraged to do research projects, and even in many cases have been discouraged from looking too closely at what goes on in their classrooms or schools, they aren't going to think of doing research. They don't know what benefits they might experience from doing a research project.

MAGGIE: Although there was somebody on that first set of answers who wanted to learn more about teacher researchers, so there's somebody who's done some reading, or been exposed to it somehow, enough to know that it's there and it sounds interesting.

SUZANNE: When we ask teachers what kind of in-service experiences they would like to have, in a sense it's still somebody from outside coming in and saying, "Well, we now believe we should involve you in planning this, but we're still in control." By asking them, we're still in control. When I read Ellen's text I wondered what would happen if we simply said, "All right, you have X amount of time for in-service over the year, you need to plan it yourselves," and just let them do it. Part of my answer was, "What do we as the 'experts' do when they say, 'Well, we just want more time to put up bulletin boards in our classrooms'"?

JERRI: With so little time, that's a reasonable kind of thing, so part of our responsibility is helping teachers see that this will be of benefit to them in some way. Then the question is, "Will it be?"

MAGGIE: And how do you know that before they go through it?

JERRI: I would imagine that you would advertise what you were doing in a way that would appeal to teachers. People may come just for points, but then gradually over time, through dialogue, through shifting the responsibility to them, they might see the possibilities of doing research. Maybe you wouldn't even mention the term *research* because research is an outsider term even if you put *teacher* in front of it. Rather than seeing the structure that we have here in Massachusetts as a problem, we could explore how to persuade teachers to look at things differently.

MAGGIE: Although you're still back to Suzanne's issue of control, which is there.

JERRI: No, no, you use the authority of the structure to create a space for persuasion. The point isn't to be philosophically consistent, but rather to get started.

ELLEN: It sounds to me like what you're suggesting is that part of the points be given right from the beginning of the planning process, that teachers be involved, which I think is a really great idea. But do we have a hidden agenda? We go in and say, "What do you want to learn?" or "How do you want to learn it?" hoping that we can convince them to do it in a way that we think is a good way. Or are we really open to anything? If they say, "I think I can improve my teaching best this year by having more time to work on the bulletin boards and learning about conflict resolution," would we bring in the consultant about that?

JERRI: It doesn't have to be either/or. You start with conflict resolution techniques, if that's where you are, but then gradually work with them to formulate questions and to focus on their classrooms rather than on techniques. I think teachers should have thousands of techniques, but have them document classrooms, set them asking questions about what they see. Gradually they come to see the importance of doing the research and reflecting on their practice.

Modes and Models of Participation

DIANE: It's not unlike any teaching experience. How do you know what the needs are? Where do you start? For new language learners, it's a question of using some kind of task, a diagnostic task, that helps to create the agenda from which to go forth. But I thought that the premise underlying this in-service was that you didn't necessarily have an ongoing evolutionary relationship with the particular group, that it's one shot. And that seems to me to be another playing field. We're invited to "come in and do this, come in and do that," where the best you can do is to find out as much as you possibly can about the context and the needs and the people and all that before your one-time visit. One thing I now do pretty consistently is refuse one-shot invitations. I will accept a two-shot invitation, which gives me the first visit to make contact and to work with people and to find out what's going on. I still have to come in with something; it's not just a dialogue. But at least the first visit gives me the opportunity to define something with them, and it also provides an opportunity for a space, an interim period, during which, if they choose, they can continue to work on what we started during the first visit. The problems that arise and whatever else surfaces can then be addressed during the second visit. With two visits there is a little better chance of having some lasting effect.

FRANCIS: One thing I was hoping we would talk about is the politics of our participation in these workshops. I've been very reluctant to do them because I haven't felt comfortable with it. Talking with teachers, they seem so disdainful of these workshops; their hackles are up; they're just very unimpressed. They're going through this because they're required to. I'm happy to hear Diane talk about a model that's been more comfortable. Are there other things we can do? Is it better politically to refuse to do these and say, "Why don't you figure out what you want to do, and do it yourself? You've got all these resources; you've got experienced people."

SUZANNE: Can we somehow suggest to administrators that this is not the way to go about it, that they need to work with teachers in order to get teachers to take some initiative in the planning, and then we're happy to be there as resources?

MAGGIE: Then you get the issue of the competition among the teachers. There have been cases where researchers have gone into schools on a regular basis and worked with teams of teachers on reflecting on their classrooms. A couple of those people rise to the top and have ongoing contact with the researchers in the university. Within certain domains that gives them a kind of prestige, and they use it to go on for an advanced degree, or they end up being the person in their school who works with other teachers. There's always a lot of jockeying for position and competition.

DIANE: While you're working on issues of reflectivity, the way in which you work can be collaborative and not competitive. You're modeling a process as well as talking about how reflectivity occurs in the classroom. The problem is that the time you spend modeling the process is so minuscule compared to the environment at the school where the competitiveness gets reinforced all the time. So another thing you can try to do is inspire people to get back in touch with what drew them into teaching in the first place, to get back in touch with what witnessing learning means for them. It may not be that I can teach reflectivity in a short time, and it may not be that we can work on collaboration in a way that's lasting, but if there's a way to get people back in touch with the excitement of learning, watching it in other people, that might launch them. Being in touch with that is the essence of teaching, and then the rest follows. Then they're eager for the tools that will allow them to continue that.

MAGGIE: So, even if you only have a one-time shot, you can get them working together around something and discussing issues that really are relevant and important. Even if they don't remember the content later, they may walk away from it saying, "Wait a minute, there is a value to getting together to talk, to start to look at some of this stuff."

JERRI: What if we, as teacher educators, were more proactive and advertised that we were interested in working with a group of teachers who want to reflect on their own teaching and have a good dialogue about it?

MAGGIE: But you're still going to get the teachers that on the survey came up with, "I want to learn more about teacher research," and you're not going to get the teachers who came up with something else.

JERRI: Well, why not? When you say, "These are the kinds of issues I'm really interested in," you're putting yourself out there, as opposed to the other way, "Here, I'm here to help you." Here you're saying, "I'm interested in working with anybody who wants to do this," as a dialogue, where we can learn from each other.

MAGGIE: It seems to me that all that does is make it much more comfortable for us. We're then able to work with the groups of teachers who want to do that, and we're not facing a room full of teachers who don't want to be there.

JERRI: We've already talked about that not being worth very much anyway, if that's the case.

MAGGIE: I don't know that it's the right attitude to just say, "Let's leave the teachers who are not interested and work with the ones where we really can accomplish something." Not that there isn't some value to taking the teachers who want to explore and learn, and see if, over time, they can spread things in their school. It's a long, slow process.

DIANE: That's a diffusion model of innovation, thinking in terms of waves as opposed to covering the whole ocean.

JERRI: This is what we did in Springfield. We started with one teacher. She was very much part of the research team, and really interesting things came out as we documented what was going on. Then we got a grant, so we were able to increase the number of teachers to 26. The "carrot" was that all the teachers in the program were given a budget to spend in their classrooms for materials, plus they got a master's degree as part of an off-campus program. We've been working with them for 2 years now. In the third year there's another budget, but they have to share it with someone in the school who is not in our program. They're going to be in a position to collaborate and work with other teachers in the same school. The original teacher I worked with, Jo-Anne, works with teachers in their classrooms, giving advice and supporting them when they try new things. So that's the design and it spreads out from there, and we imagine that eventually teachers themselves can take on the whole thing.

MAGGIE: Weren't you working with Jo-Anne for a couple of years, even before the grants, when the administration came to you and said, "You're doing good things, can we disseminate it somehow?" What made them willing to invest in this project? I think there are a lot of school districts where you would have had resistance and where that might not have happened.

JERRI: One of the things that happened is that when you work and you're open and you let people see what you're doing, suddenly you get the teachers looking and saying, "Oh, what's going on?" Then you have the administrators looking in and seeing what's going on. And when people see things and think, "Oh, wow, this is interesting," they want to become part of it. Gradually the superintendent did the same thing.

DIANE: But that's after you were present.

JERRI: Yes, but it's not exactly accurate that it was us who went in there with one teacher and it spread. The school itself was slowly becoming a whole-language school. Jo-Anne was one of the teachers in the school. They had formed study groups, they had done other things, so when we came in, it was not the beginning of a new culture. There was a culture there already. Then we started working with Jo-Anne and everybody became very interested in what was going on. Maggie raises a good point, however. I think you have to be there in order to see when the opportunities arise. By staying on campus waiting for people to come to you, you're definitely not going to know when the time is ripe.

MAGGIE: The school was ready, but that was combined with your very visible presence in the school.

JERRI: Well, we are the ones who enabled it to spread out to other teachers because we write grants all the time; we know grant language. The grant foundation said that our proposal was much more sophisticated than the other grants that the schools put in, so they definitely got the grant because we were there. It's a symbiotic relationship. The question is how do you get that going? You have to be there. You have to be there to see what the possibilities are in that particular place.

FRANCIS: It seems to me that your project is directly relevant to something we were talking about before. That teacher you first started to work with was a first-grade teacher who had just gotten her doctorate. She was the perfect liaison between two cultures: She had been socialized to the university culture, and she had vast experience with elementary schools. That gave you some validity, that it wasn't you coming in purveying this new approach; it was really a teacher working in the system who was excited by this.

JERRI: Oh, I think that's important. Although I don't think it necessarily has to be a doctoral student, just someone with that kind of interest and willingness to reflect and engage with new ideas.

DIANE: One of the most successful in-service models I know of is the one that's been ongoing in Italy for a number of years now. The Fulbright Commission has had primary responsibility for it. Teachers nominate themselves, and if they are selected after an interview, they come to the United States for a 6-week period. They have a methodology course and a few other courses, but half of the 6-week period is spent on their taking the material that has been presented to them and their own ideas, and creating syllabi. Then they take those syllabi and go back to Italy. In return for having this trip to the United States, they have to spend 2 years conducting in-service workshops for their colleagues. The ministry of education was supportive as well, so there were points awarded for colleagues attending the in-service courses. This was a perfect marriage, I think, because these people were intimately acquainted with the context in which they were working, they knew the clientele, they knew the problems so well, that they could take the material they were being exposed to and fashion it in a way that was useful. The results have been amazing. Italy went from a very grammar-centered, grammar-translation approach to language teaching to a communicative approach largely because of this program.

SUZANNE: I did a similar thing in a summer institute in Connecticut, where the state provides money for summer courses and the teachers get in-service points. The teachers had to take what they had learned in the week-long session with me back to their schools. Then we met again in January to report back. A lot of the whole language in a certain area of Connecticut is traced back to a week that I spent down there many years ago. So the model of requiring them to go back into their schools with the information they have works very well.

Social and Institutional Structures

FRANCIS: It's interesting that all the models we've discussed have that as an integral element, even though in Jerri's case, she actually works in a school site, and in Diane's model, people are being extracted from their context. But all these models have this idea of diffusion as fundamental to how the real change is going to take place.

DIANE: The critical notion is that the agents are from the culture itself.

MAGGIE: But what happens when a teacher changes but the culture of the school doesn't? Say you have 30 people in a class for a semester, and over time they buy into certain kinds of philosophies or methodologies. But then individually they go back into their schools and they are the only ones who believe in this. What happens then? They go back into a culture that's not accepting of it, and what do they do? Do they stick with what they've just done for 3 months in a college classroom, or do they go back to the culture of the school? Do you need a culture, and peers and colleagues to do it with, even if it's only a small minority of the teachers who are going to support you? Do you need a critical mass? What does it take to provide the support?

DIANE: We saw something that worked very well in Italy, which addresses your questions. If you don't have the critical mass in the culture of your school, you could actually, as part of your model, create a new culture. That's essentially what they did in Italy. After the teachers returned and worked in their in-service capacity, they were given leave time from their schools to get together periodically as trainers. From time to time, those of us who had been doing methodology courses with them in this country were brought over to attend those centralized meetings, and also to travel around and work with people. We know that you need to keep it alive for people, otherwise it does disappear.

FRANCIS: Maybe we could think about it in terms of social structure. You need to create some kind of learning community within a school or a school district. Maybe we can provide support for that, and one important piece of support is money, grant writing. So we introduce these models that we've been talking about and say, "You know, there are ways of doing in-service work other than paying somebody to come in; you can look at this diffusion model." So we might help people conceptualize how they can move forward. When you've got the range of topics that Ellen has chronicled here, what do you do with that? Maybe rather than trying to figure out a good topic, you help people organize themselves.

JERRI: I think one of the difficulties in schools is that there isn't a culture that fosters talking together about teaching. In our project we used teamwork, and what teachers commented on was how exciting and interesting it was being able to talk to other teachers and having that time together.

MAGGIE: That's why I said earlier that maybe one of the things you can do in a one-time shot is to make teachers realize how valuable it is to be able to get together and talk and share. And then you're already starting to create a climate where that's valued.

DIANE: You can't do it in a one-shot model, but if you launch the process, that's part of the inspiration. We also have to remember that in any model that is likely to meet with success you have to entertain a long-term commitment. Change takes a long time, and it may never happen.

FRANCIS: If a learning community of teachers comes together, and they invite you, and you do your two workshops, they are the continuity; Diane's not the continuity. She comes in and provides inspiration, information, whatever. It seems like such a different model than you coming and organizing the group and doing it. So, one thing I might ask is, "Is this group meeting on a regular basis, or is this group just forming for me to come in and do my workshop and then disbanding?" I might be interested in playing a small role in an ongoing process rather than being the whole show.

MAGGIE: I think we're cycling right back to where the whole conversation started. You've got teachers who have been in the classroom 20 years, who are certified high school English teachers grandfathered into ESL,[2] who are doing ESL because they were forced into doing it, not by choice, but there they are. They still think that they know what they're doing, they're sensitive, they're caring, they know the English language, they're teaching these kids, they're doing fine. Now all of a sudden they find out that they're not grandfathered any more, and someone's telling them to go to this workshop. What do we do? We have a personal right to say, "I'm not going to work with them; it's not going to do any good." But that's not doing the kids they're teaching any good.

ELLEN: If you care about the kids and the classrooms, you can't say, "This is not a good person to work with." Can we really do triage here? "Well, this one-third is too sick to be worth saving, so we'll just sweep them under the rug. This other one-third is so good, thank goodness we don't need to work with them." Then we'll find the ones that are just right to work with. There may be some sense to that, but you always know in the back of your mind that there are people you can't reach or choose not to reach, or who don't want to

---

[2] Many states that did not have ESL certification designated other certificates (e.g., English or foreign languages) that would enable teachers to legally teach ESL. Often when the states did adopt ESL certification, those teachers remained grandfathered as certified ESL teachers, even though they had no training in ESL teaching.

be reached, and they have kids in their classrooms. There's a pressure about that.

DIANE: I had a thought. It might be interesting to treat a workshop, a one-shot or two-shot deal, as a launch pad for independent studies. What I can do is help provide a structure for you. You choose the topic, and then I will help you to structure it, provide resources or whatever I can do to help you research it, and the deal is that you have to pay back. The next time we come together, you'll be given 5 minutes, 10 minutes, to talk about what you've learned about that topic. Rather than going in there with a preset agenda, or fishing for one, or even negotiating one, make it their agenda, but the process is what you contribute. This might be another way to deal with topics that they are interested in.

JERRI: However, there is still the issue about selectivity and how it's framed. In our project, we didn't get diverse faculty volunteering. It took some recruitment, it took framing the project in a way that made sense to a variety of different people.

FRANCIS: I heard an African-American woman talk about being asked to work with a group of students who were the first African-American students to be enrolled in a particular program. They wanted her to find out what the students wanted and to make them comfortable. Her first response was to ask them, "How come it took so long?" Then she said, "You know, I think members of the group that you've selected are probably very good at dealing with white culture. What I'd like to do is work with your faculty." That makes me think. When somebody invites us into a school system to do a workshop, what if we said, "All right, but we want to work with the administrators." We're saying it's an institutional issue, that no workshop is going to help because it takes institutional structure to change things. What if we made it more explicit who is deficient? Is it really the teachers? It can't be the teachers all the time.

SUZANNE: That's the piece that's been missing here. We've been talking about the culture of the school as an abstract thing that just exists, but that's not right. It's created, and it can be changed. And I'm convinced that administrators have a very strong role in creating that culture. It's the principal who sets the tone of the school.

MAGGIE: That's why I asked Jerri about being invited by administration to come in and spread out and do what she did.

SUZANNE: When you have a school culture that's open to teacher inquiry and reflectivity, that's fostered by the administration. It doesn't happen by itself. So, the next time we're invited to do a one-shot workshop, we say, "I don't want the teachers, I want the administrators."

MAGGIE: And I want at least two shots.

DIANE: I want it to be voluntary. I want there to be a pay-off for the teachers.

MAGGIE: There's the perfect future for this group. We'll turn into a consulting group and put out a list of what we can do and what our conditions are, and get it out to all the school districts and principals.

RESPONSE

Ken Pransky

I have been teaching ESL at an elementary school in western Massachusetts for 10 years. We have a strong staff very interested in professional growth, with a good staff development program. However, we have been grappling with a rapidly changing student population at a time of reduced levels of funding, increased mandates, and increasing public skepticism. The administration generates the topics of our mandated in-service curriculum days without much teacher input. My comments are based on this experience, in addition to conversations I have had with teachers from other districts over the years.

First, I question an important assumption I sensed in the article and in your discussion, namely, that all teachers must equally value professional reflection and change. I think those values must be learned and nurtured.

They become part of teacher discourse (*Discourse* as defined by Gee, 1996) for those teachers who were trained to see them as integral to good teaching. Teachers who were trained and began work in a different educational landscape may well have first experienced reflection and change when an administrator tried to shake things up. To these teachers, reflection may seem dangerous, somehow an admission of poor performance, a potential source of friction with administration, or even a cause for punitive action. We should not assume that all teachers value professional reflection in the same way, though it may be true for a growing number of more recently trained teachers.

Second, mandatory in-services generated from the top with little or no teacher input are very frustrating for teachers. They rarely deal with real teacher priorities and can even make a teacher's job more complicated and stressful. They have come to symbolize an increasing loss of professional autonomy, strengthening the negative feelings that many teachers already have. In some districts where this is a serious problem, in-services sometimes serve as a battleground where teachers and administrators vie for control.

Another force driving top-down teacher in-services is what I call administrator prerogative. Such in-services develop out of administrators' educational biases or philosophies. Of course, these may not match what their staffs think is good educational practice or how they assess their own classroom needs. Unless administrators have asked teachers about their needs and responded to them, teachers forced to attend such in-services will feel very put-upon.

Educational fads can also drive in-service programs, with some school systems lurching from fad to fad. Teachers get superficial training in something, the school system neither supports teachers in it nor nurtures its use, and then the next thing comes along. Administrators who mandate one-shot overviews of new ideas without offering ongoing support or resources also frustrate teachers.

Nevertheless, when administrators observe real needs, they are responsible for properly analyzing them and initiating in-service programs. Some school systems engage in numerous questionable practices with uniformly poor educational results. Administrators have a responsibility to the students to insist on whatever training they believe their staff needs. But whatever changes are needed, administrators must involve teachers in developing the programs. The system must also commit the time, resources, and support mechanisms necessary to initiate and then nurture the changes. Absent a glaring, systemwide need, I think staff from individual schools should develop their own in-service professional development agenda with administrative consultation and support. Teachers need the time to collaborate, support for taking risks in the classroom, and the resources necessary to carry out their programs effectively. As your discussion reflected, teachers need professional and/or financial incentives to encourage them to engage in this process and to reinforce their status as respected professionals. When administration approaches teachers supportively, as competent professionals, and asks them to analyze student needs and devise a teacher training program to meet those needs, most teachers will respond in kind, without mistrust or cynicism.

I believe that before an outside expert accepts a contract to conduct an in-service, he or she should clearly state what resources (e.g., time and money) will be required to meet the in-service's goals. The expert should outline his or her recommendations in a public document so that teachers will know what the administration must do to create a successful program. If the administrator cannot provide these resources, then the expert should not conduct the in-service. In this field, half-a-loaf can be even worse for teachers and students than no loaf at all because administrators expect teachers to get optimal results with the resources provided, sufficient or not. In our district, for example, we decided last year to untrack many secondary classes, which entailed training teachers to work with heterogeneous groups. The trainer told the mathematics department that such groupings do not work well when classes have more than 16 or 18 students. This year, however, some math classes have as many as 27 students! Nevertheless, parents and administrators expect teachers to work with heterogeneous groups in these larger classes.

Along with recommending resources, the expert should also delineate any necessary administrative changes. Teachers would likely welcome clearly stated performance expectations for administrators because it would shift the burden for change from their shoulders to the entire system.

I like very much the in-service models that Diane, Jerri, and Suzanne mentioned in their discussion. Skeptical or resistant teachers would more likely accept a new idea or way of working when a school or a district has a critical mass of energized, excited teachers who have made the idea their own. If I identify something that actually works for me in the classroom, another teacher with similar concerns will likely become interested. Teachers are far more open to energized colleagues than to administrators.

Training is more likely to be successful when teachers are engaged in needs assessment and developing in-service agendas as long as administration provides the time, resources, and other support needed for a program to be successful. Outside experts can shape productive in-service experiences by outlining their recommendations in a public document and refusing to accept inferior conditions. It is welcome indeed when this process helps a staff rethink and revise its priorities and programs to enhance the quality of teaching. The most successful training occurs when groups of committed teachers excite their colleagues with real results.

REFERENCES

Gee, J. P. (1996). *Social linguistics and literacies: Ideology in discourse.* London: Taylor & Francis.

Lange, J. D., & Burroughs-Lange, S. (1994, April). *Professional uncertainty and professional growth.* Paper presented at the American Educational Research Association Conference, New Orleans, LA.

PROMOTING FURTHER CONVERSATIONS

Clair, N., & Adger, C. T. (2000). Sustainable strategies for professional development in education reform. In K. Johnson (Ed.), *Teacher education* (pp. 11–27). Alexandria, VA: TESOL.

Diaz-Maggioli, G. H. (2003). *Professional development for language teachers.* Washington, DC: Center for Applied Linguistics. Retrieved January 19, 2003, from http://www.cal.org/resources /digest/0303diaz.html. (ERIC Digest No. EDO-FL-03–03)

Gonzalez, J. M., & Darling-Hammond, L. (1997). *New concepts for new challenges: Professional development for teachers of immigrant youth. Topics in Immigrant Education: Vol. 2.* McHenry, IL: Delta Systems, & Washington, DC: Center for Applied Linguistics.

Head, K., & Taylor, P. (1997). *Readings in teacher development.* New York: Macmillan.

Roberts, S. M., & Pruitt, E. Z. (2003). *Schools as professional learning communities: Collaborative activities and strategies for professional development.* Thousand Oaks, CA: Sage.

3

Controlling a
Negotiated Syllabus

TEXT

Suzanne Irujo

The move from a traditional transmission model of learning to a more collaborative, learner-centered model has forced us as teacher educators to reexamine the often contradictory roles that we and our students play. We must encourage our students to rely on their own expertise, allow them to discover and construct their own knowledge and practice, and support them as they learn for themselves how to be teachers; at the same time, we must acknowledge that we, as teacher educators, are the experts they expect; we possess the specific knowledge and skills that our students must acquire, and we are the gatekeepers who will judge their readiness to become teachers. We might want our students to explore areas of interest to them, engage in activities that they feel will be useful, and participate in evaluating how well they are doing, but our institutions require that we include certain materials in our courses, ensure that our students meet certain competencies, and evaluate their teaching abilities.

One way to ease the tensions that these contradictory roles create is to use a negotiated or process syllabus, which allows students to help determine the content, procedures, and requirements of their courses. In my case, the negotiation began by chance, when the syllabus I had prepared for my methodology class did not begin to meet the needs of the students, who that year were mostly experienced teachers. We began rewriting the syllabus spontaneously during the first class meeting, and for the rest of the semester these students seemed to be more involved in their own learning than students in previous classes had been. They read widely from a variety of sources, and they chose assignments that they felt would be most useful to them. Although their greater maturity no doubt accounts in part for their active participation, I wanted to believe that they were also more involved because they had a voice in determining course requirements.

The class had one dissenting voice that first year, a student who was very reserved for most of the semester. She later told me that she had first reacted to the class very negatively. She expected teachers to tell students what to do; because I had not done that, she felt that I must not be a good teacher. This was the first of numerous clashes between what students expected teachers' and students' roles to be and my desire to change those roles. As the negotiation process became a planned part of the course, I modified the process each year to try to overcome student resistance. What follows is a brief summary of what we did and how the students responded (for a more complete account of how the negotiation process changed from year to year, see Irujo, 2000).

The first year I actually planned to negotiate the syllabus, I had a very small class. I decided to simply ask the students what they would like to learn, but they met this question with blank stares and complete silence. They did not know enough about the field even to begin to suggest course content. Back to the drawing board.

Another year I began with no syllabus but explained why students should help in developing it, and I led the students in a brainstorming activity designed to help them focus on their own language learning experiences. They then filled out a questionnaire about what they would like to learn, how they thought they could best learn it, and how they would like to be evaluated. The students and I used the questionnaires to synthesize the syllabus. That process seemed to go smoothly, but the international students were uncomfortable with the whole idea. They wanted me to tell them what to read and what assignments to do; one student asked for a list of readings for all the topics that the syllabus would have covered if we had not negotiated it. In addition, students seemed to choose the easiest assignments rather than the ones that would be most helpful for them, and I worried that they might give themselves unjustified grades. I also worried about certification competencies that were not included on the syllabus and about student resistance eroding my belief in the benefits of the negotiating process.

Another year I decided to take a more active role by including certain topics on the syllabus and requiring a teaching unit as a final project, although individuals could get permission to do other projects. I strongly recommended peer teaching and dialogue journals, and I included my evaluation as well as theirs in computing grades. The questionnaire that students filled out was much more detailed, with a list of possible topics and suggestions for assignments and activities. This strategy did not work at all; everybody wanted to do everything, and negotiating a consensus took a great deal of time. The syllabus that emerged was almost exactly the same as what I would have developed myself, and some students complained that the process took too long. I also became concerned as the semester went along that once the syllabus was completed, the negotiating process stopped. After the negotiated syllabus was typed up and handed out, it functioned in exactly the same way as a traditional syllabus, serving as a road map for what we were supposed to do, with no thought of renegotiating it as needed.

Another year, another large class, this one more diverse than ever. Feeling a little discouraged, I simply developed a syllabus myself, traditional in all respects except that it listed a variety of textbooks from which students could choose. Having done some reading in which the term *process syllabus* was used instead of *negotiated syllabus,* I presented it as the first draft and invited students to suggest changes. They suggested very few changes at first, but as we went along, students felt free to make suggestions about how we were spending class time, how their assignments should be evaluated, and the form of their final projects. International students and more traditional students felt comfortable using the draft as a guide and were not upset about a perceived lack of direction. I could also stipulate that certain topics and requirements were nonnegotiable, thus enabling me to stop worrying about the expert and gatekeeper aspects of my contradictory roles. It seemed that at last I had developed a procedure that would allow me to practice what I preach: The process encouraged students to plan their own learning, met the needs of diverse students, and allowed students to observe and engage in reflective teaching as together we periodically reviewed goals, content, procedures, and evaluation. And I could do all that without feeling that I had imposed my views on students who might have very different ideas about how learning best occurs.

Another year, a smaller class, a feeling of optimism. For the first time in years I did not change the process of constructing the syllabus. When students didn't suggest changes to the syllabus in the beginning, I didn't worry. When they didn't suggest changes as we got further into the course, however, I did begin to worry. And when, in spite of my encouragement, they didn't ever suggest changes, I began to wonder. Although students did not resist the process, they did not seem to be engaged, either. The students did good work, enjoyed the class, and claimed that they had learned a lot. The course evaluations were the best I had ever received. Maybe I should just stop worrying.

I return to one of the paradoxes that we discussed in our early meetings: Don't we have to control certain processes to allow students to take control themselves? How can we get them to take responsibility for their own learning without forcing them to accept our view of the learning process?

CONVERSATION

The conversation began with Suzanne emphasizing that no matter how the negotiation was done, the goals were always the same: to give students input into what they were reading, what the course requirements were, and how assignments would be graded. The discussion continued with questions and clarifications about procedures, such as how Suzanne presented the idea of negotiation and how decisions were made.

Reasons to Negotiate a Syllabus

> DIANE: I've negotiated the syllabus with my linguistics class for 8 or 9 years now; the students are experienced teachers, and I feel I can't pretend to know what they need to work on. I ask them to pick out

a dozen topics, recognizing that not all of them are going to make it on the syllabus, and I have them vote. To me it's time well spent. It's important not just so the course itself is relevant to my students' needs, but also because this is exactly the way I want them to work with their own students—to find out what it is their own students need. It's both a way of making my course relevant and a modeling of a process. We do revisit the choice of topics from time to time during the course. The other thing is that I haven't negotiated the process; I do just the content.

SUZANNE: I came to terms with the content issue early on. There are certain competencies students have to have for certification, and some of them are supposed to be done in my methodology course. It was not a difficult decision to say that certain things are nonnegotiable. They have to be. I have to know that my students can do certain things, and part of the reason I negotiate both content and process is to give them options for how they show me what they can do. Maybe the experienced teachers can just go and do a set of sequential lesson plans and bring them in to me. They don't have to do the readings and all the things that the undergraduates have to do in order to learn this. So process is intertwined with content in order to have the content meet the needs of very diverse students.

FRANCIS: One of the things I've been thinking about is that in a negotiated syllabus, the message they're getting may not be the message you're intending. If you say, "We're going to negotiate this syllabus; I want you to be invested in what you're learning, I want you to have some input into that," and you don't open it up to the full complexity of where you're standing, of what you're going to negotiate, you're doing them a disservice. You're reducing it down as if everything were negotiable, when really there are certain parts that aren't. The negotiation part is that you have to justify it. You have to be open to question and critique on your decision that some items are nonnegotiable, that there are certain things that have to be from your point of view.

DIANE: I certainly understand why you would say that some things are not negotiable. I did it too, saying "this is not negotiable," and, by implication, all else is. That's a good reason to exert your authority, to say what's on the table and what's off limits. But on the other hand, that's really giving a mixed message, isn't it? Why do we invite negotiation in the first place? If it's because students need to have a say in their own educational process and content, and there's an empowering payoff to that, then why would we not want to put everything up for discussion if they could make a reasonable case for it?

Successful Negotiation

SUZANNE: I've wondered what made the negotiation more successful in some years than in others, and I don't see any patterns. Maybe it only takes one or two people who come with a different perspective. They might not necessarily be the older, more experienced teachers, but one or two who have a different perspective will vocalize that, and this sparks the others. But if you're missing that one or two, the others don't seem to pick up on it from my suggestions.

JERRI: I wonder if it doesn't have something to do with your own attitude towards it? When it's spontaneous you're responding to something from the students rather than imposing, so the task is different. We might be able to explore what that means in terms of working or not working.

ELLEN: When the negotiation of the syllabus comes spontaneously, because the syllabus doesn't fit the needs of the students, then the whole process becomes much more authentic.

DIANE: You're saying that it's very empowering if students see that you're responding to their needs on the spot, as opposed to coming in and saying, "I want to empower you; your assignment is to make yourselves empowered."

JERRI: An underlying current here in a lot of the comments is the idea that what you're aiming for is something that makes everybody happy, that it all works out and there are no problems. The basic concern here seems to be that something didn't work. I think we should explore what we mean by "it didn't work." While students may resist, they are being exposed to the principles and ideas behind negotiated learning. Later on, many of them may evaluate their experiences in your classroom differently. I think you saw that in Tom, who was certainly not satisfied [see chapter 1]. Over time he began to think about it more, precisely because he wasn't satisfied. Not being satisfied may in some ways be a motivator to continue thinking.

SUZANNE: So it may be that even if they don't participate in the process at the time, they've seen me making it available to them, they've heard my reasons for doing it, and it may stick. Although if they don't participate in it, if they don't experience it, how will it stick in their minds, how will they remember?

DIANE: But they have experienced it!

SUZANNE: Have they, if they haven't responded at all?

MAGGIE: They haven't actually experienced negotiating the syllabus because they didn't negotiate it. It wasn't negotiated. But they've experienced someone trying to engage them in the process.

DIANE: If James O'Toole [1996] is right that the only way to overcome resistance is for people to develop an alternative belief system and make it their own, we can't expect that it's going to happen within the course of a semester. If it happens within their lifetime, we're doing pretty well. So if you're in the education business, you're a risk taker of that sort because learning isn't going to happen immediately. The other thing would be to have faith in students, that they understand that you are acting out of some conviction.

JERRI: Not only acting out of your convictions, but also articulating them consistently throughout. So later when students begin to understand what you were trying to do, they also have the memory of your articulation of the process. That articulation helps them make sense of the experience. Experience without articulation would make it more difficult to understand later.

ELLEN: So what happens is that when students are obviously not happy with the way the course is going, that can always become material for the course.

JERRI: Right. A negotiated syllabus needs to be more than a negotiated syllabus. It also needs to be a process of understanding the role that negotiation plays in learning and teaching more generally. Choosing topics is only one aspect. Yes, topics that appear more relevant to the student are more likely to be interesting. But students also need to understand that negotiation is always occurring and needs to occur if students are to learn.

Types of Negotiation

FRANCIS: Could you argue that any syllabus is negotiated in reality? I'm thinking of the sense in which you prepare a syllabus for a class and you say, "This is how we're going to work things." But the students begin to select what they read, what they pay attention to, how they do the assignments. There's always this level of negotiation.

JERRI: That was my experience when I first started teaching at U. Mass. [University of Massachusetts]. I had teachers who had worked all day coming into class and they would just sit there, rolling their eyes, no matter what I did. Because of their reactions, I changed. If any learning was to occur, it had to be active. That experience has been the basis for everything I do in my classes today. So in a way, it was negotiated. [For a description of Jerri's courses at the University of Massachusetts, Amherst, see chapter 1].

FRANCIS: We're talking about two kinds of negotiation, one is inter-active and the other is a formal mechanism where you set up a process.

SUZANNE: I think the formal process is important because it brings the process to awareness. A lot of students don't realize that what you do is a result of how they're reacting to it. You could go through a whole semester, and they would never know that you had been negotiating the whole time. By doing the formal process, they become aware of it and are more likely to engage in it.

DIANE: When I was at UCLA [University of California, Los Angeles] I taught a course in introductory Indonesian. Students were learning the language and satisfying the language requirement, but it was designed for language teachers and teachers-to-be, and they were supposed to be learning about language teaching from it. One of the things I asked them to do was to keep a log of what we did and to figure out why they thought we did that. And they would ascribe to me reasons why I did things that wouldn't ever have occurred to me! Their reasons were theoretically sound and very coherent. It was wonderful. And then we'd have discussions about them. It seems that this might be a very interesting technique for looking at the theory and practice connections in my own classroom. Usually, I only explain why I'm doing something when I meet with resistance and people need an explanation. But I don't necessarily do it when things are going smoothly. It might be fun to have people document activities and ask them why they think we're doing it.

MAGGIE: It's one of those things where if you start out by being explicit, by saying "Here's what I'm going to do, here's why I'm going to do it," it wouldn't have much impact anyway. It has to arise out of a real problem, a real tension that needs to be addressed, where people have some reason to be focused on and interested in that particular issue. Or as Diane suggests, if they're documenting it and coming up with it, and that's what leads to the discussion, that's different than if you just lay it out at the very beginning of the process.

FRANCIS: A lot of negotiations in my classes happen when things come to a head, when there's a problem, and things break down. Often it's around ambiguity, that I give an assignment and I don't specify exactly what I want. I'll set something up for students to do and not specify what's supposed to happen. For example, one time last fall, I said, "Let's create a dialogue, and we'll make one person responsible for a piece of it." We were working with verb tenses or something like that. It was just too ambiguous, and afterward, students came to me and said, "I was unhappy about this; I was put on the spot; I really didn't understand what you wanted me to do." From that, we were able to renegotiate the roles in the class. We had a very interesting discussion about roles and what my expectations were. They responded with what they needed, and we negotiated something quite different. We didn't change the content of the course, but we negotiated the process that we were involved in. There was a very different feeling from that time on. It took students' coming to me and saying, "We're not happy with something. We want the roles better defined." The students had to see that the teacher would respond to this, but there was also a kind of emotional thing, where we all went through this. After that we were all open to seeing different ways of working together and seeing the whole point of this: that we're going to work together. It happened again in the spring, and now I'm beginning to think it's almost like manipulation, that I'm structuring opportunities for us to have this big blow-out because it's so productive.

Self-Doubts

MAGGIE: Does this mean that we have to manipulate people or force them to go through certain things in order to accomplish our goals?

SUZANNE: That's something I worry about. I think it has to do with a fear of imposing on others. Although I really believe in what I'm doing, there's a part of me that thinks I'm imposing my own beliefs on students who could very legitimately have different beliefs.

JERRI: There's more to it than just belief. It's a theory-based belief, and that's one of the things that's difficult to get across to students. But it's important for them to understand that these are theoretically based decisions, even if sometimes in the process of implementing them they don't go as they should.

SUZANNE: But there are plenty of other people who don't accept the theories I believe in. When I think about that, a little voice pops up and says, "What if they're right, and I'm wrong?" But the part of me that questions my beliefs is very small. It's actually a positive thing because it keeps me continually reassessing my beliefs and reaffirming them. When that little voice pops up, I have to stop and look at what I'm doing and say, "Well, yes, I really do believe in this. I'm going to go on doing the kinds of things I've been doing because I really do believe it." So it's a good thing to have.

ELLEN: In a way, you have to think like that. There's never a place where you can become complacent and say, "I have discovered the right way to do this. It always works. I never have to worry about it again." If we don't worry about the possibility that we could be wrong, then we stop growing as teachers and as human beings.

RESPONSE

Avrom Feinberg

Thank you for the opportunity to become involved in your project. It is very fitting that you have chosen this conversation for my response. I find that the negotiated approach keeps subject matter pertinent for students, allows for appropriate changes in guidelines without sacrificing learning goals, and enables students to own their final product.

I was negotiated in a curriculum development class that Suzanne taught in Ecuador, where I was teaching sixth grade, in English, to a class of Ecuadorian students whose English skills were fairly limited. I approached many of my classes with a preplanned curriculum. I moved through specific subject matter on the Savanna or Brazil or whatever pertained to the week's geography lesson. As the year progressed, my planning sessions with fellow teachers consisted of researching units, discussing students' reading assignments, and creating ways for the students to explore the topic that we chose. We created grammar or vocabulary lessons weeks before actually teaching them in class. As teachers, we provided students with easy access to the materials that we wanted them to use. Our students remained busy, yet were they truly engaged and excited about their work?

As a result of Suzanne's class, I began teaching my middle school students using techniques similar to those that she had modeled for our master's level group. I began with a simple writing assignment: I asked students to choose a subject and explore it through writing. As a class we developed the schedule, a progression toward a final publication date. As students wrestled with describing their world in new ways, I taught grammar lessons and introduced vocabulary as the need arose. I provided them with the tools for their own learning. Along with my team (an ESL specialist who worked in my classroom, my counterpart who worked with a separate section of sixth-grade students, and the head of the middle school who was studying with Suzanne as well), I created a classroom environment that responded to students' interests and needs, which gave them access to their own learning.

When I moved from Ecuador and became an English teacher at a private school in Colorado, I realized how well the construction and negotiation process would work for teaching middle school students. After using the student-directed approach for our first writing project, I moved on to more complex and involved negotiations. When I teach reading and writing, I now prefer that the students have some reason for their work so that they feel learning English is important to them.

To guide our year's studies, we as a school chose the theme of community. With my seventh and eighth graders, I suggested that we design an interpretive tape for a drive up a river valley to a mountain north of our town. This tape would be used by visitors to the area to interpret the natural landscape they were traveling through. We planned the tape to synchronize with mile markers and the natural landscape of rural northwest Colorado; listeners would be guided by our voices during their drive through the region. The students immediately jumped on the opportunity to develop their own project. I had guided their planning and procedures for previous projects, so they had experience with this process. They began this project with more energy than all of the other projects combined, however, because they were being allowed to negotiate all the steps toward their own success.

The students were involved in the creation of their own learning from the beginning of the project. They decided that they wanted their tape to have original music, historical facts, local anecdotes, legends, and ecological points of interest. We negotiated weekly assignments, including my own as teacher and project leader. Students' assignments ranged from visiting the library and interviewing local experts to writing dialogue and composing an original score. As the teacher, I was assigned to arrange transportation for a scouting drive, edit material according to deadlines, and create a makeshift sound studio in our computer lab.

Throughout the process, certain aspects of the project were nonnegotiable. Each student had to complete an assignment each week. Each student had to turn in written work with appropriate bibliographies and references. Above all, each student had to participate in planning and implementing our negotiations. As a result, the interpretive tape drove our explorations into the English language.

Our negotiated project allowed each student to approach learning with his or her own type of enthusiasm. Additionally, each student depended on his or her peers for support to finish the project in a timely and professional manner. As a teacher, I was able to use each step toward completing the tape to reach my educational goals. Throughout the process I taught organizational skills, note taking, grammar, punctuation, spelling, research, citations, tone and voice, and even music and drama. The students exceeded my expectations in accepting my goals for our English class.

When Suzanne approached me to write about the process of negotiating a syllabus, I immediately thought about our interpretive tape. As a teacher of middle school students, I couldn't use the same negotiation and facilitation process described in your conversation, if for no other reason than that very few middle-level teachers use a syllabus to organize their classes. However, by combining the negotiating process with a constructivist approach, I have bridged the gap between students' interests and my educational objectives. Students have become invested in their learning not for the sake of grades, but because their voices and their research will be available in the public domain through the copies that will be distributed to the school community.

Throughout the process, students looked to me to lead and to maintain the negotiation structure. I was able to steer them away from previously comfortable learning styles and introduce them to newer ways of gathering and presenting information. Furthermore, the project allowed all students to work with their particular strengths as writers, artists, musicians, or researchers with peer support during the process. The group's success depended on each member's work.

I have found that the negotiating process can certainly be adapted for younger students. Middle school students need to feel that they own their learning. At a time when everything seems so out of control, they need to feel they can control what enters their minds. Students who are becoming teenagers are often motivated by social stimuli and desires. By allowing students to negotiate their own learning, I have given them opportunities to be social about topics that are important to them.

College students use a course syllabus to guide their learning. It helps them to prepare for certain learning experiences and to understand the class's learning progression. However, a formal syllabus covering an entire course is developmentally inappropriate for students in middle school classes, where they work on a unit-to-unit, week-to-week, or sometimes even a day-to-day basis. Middle school teachers and students do not so much negotiate the syllabus as manipulate the content. Middle school curriculum has gradually moved away from a content-based, what-your-sixth-grader-needs-to-know approach toward a framework of skills that students need to master before moving on to high school. I now strive to enable students to own the content through which they will learn those skills.

REFERENCES

Irujo, S. (2000). A process syllabus in a methodology course: Experiences, beliefs, challenges. In M. P. Breen & A. Littlejohn (Eds.), *Classroom decision-making: Negotiation and process syllabuses in practice* (pp. 209–222). Cambridge, England: Cambridge University Press.

O'Toole, J. (1996). *Leading change: The argument for values-based leadership.* San Francisco: Jossey-Bass.

PROMOTING FURTHER CONVERSATIONS

Clarke, D. F. (1991). The negotiated syllabus: What is it and how is it likely to work? *Applied Linguistics, 12,* 13–28.

Ivanic, R. (2000). Negotiation, process, content and participants' experience in a process syllabus for ELT professionals. In M. P. Breen & A. Littlejohn (Eds.), *Classroom decision-making: Negotiation and process syllabuses in practice* (pp. 233–247). Cambridge, England: Cambridge University Press.

McCarthy, M., & Makosch, M. (2000). Discourse, process and reflection in teacher education. In M. P. Breen & A. Littlejohn (Eds.), *Classroom decision-making: Negotiation and process syllabuses in practice* (pp. 223–232). Cambridge, England: Cambridge University Press.

Nunan, D. (1988). *The learner-centered curriculum.* Cambridge, England: Cambridge University Press.

Wolfe-Quintero, K. (2000). Negotiation as a participatory dialogue. In M. P. Breen & A. Littlejohn (Eds.), *Classroom decision-making: Negotiation and process syllabuses in practice* (pp. 248–271). Cambridge, England: Cambridge University Press.

4

The Nature of Linguistics in a Language Teacher Education Program

TEXT

Diane Larsen-Freeman

A new role for linguistics in language-teacher education? Rather than reject linguistics (and other disciplines) outright, I think it is incumbent upon language-teacher educators to help teachers (and I include teacher trainees) alter the nature of their relationship with linguistics and other disciplines. This process will be assisted in three ways. First of all, teachers must learn to see linguistics as a resource to be drawn on, but not the purveyor of all facts germane to the content of their teaching. Furthermore, teachers are not mere recipients of "received wisdom" from linguists. The relationship between teachers and linguists should be construed as a lateral, nonhierarchical one. Of course, merely saying this does not make it so. One way in which this attitude can be encouraged is to expose teachers to a variety of different linguistic approaches and to play the doubting and believing games with each (Larsen-Freeman 1983b). In this way the relative strengths and weaknesses of the different approaches will become apparent. Teachers need to cultivate a consumer mentality. We need not be dictated to by others.

Second, language-teacher educators need to recognize that what linguistics has to offer lies at least as much in the areas of awareness and attitude as it does in knowledge (Larsen-Freeman 1983a). This seems especially true of the hyphenated linguistics of ethno-, socio-, and psycho-linguistics, but is no less true of what I am calling mainstream linguistics. I have found that questions work best to raise teachers' awareness and to encourage them to examine their attitudes in the context of linguistics: What does it mean to communicate? What is a language and how does it differ from a dialect? What is a word? What are the components of language and how do they interact? What does it mean to be a native speaker? How does the way language is used among native speakers vary? What does grammatical mean? What does appropriate mean? How is appropriateness determined, i.e., by whose standards? These questions and others help teacher trainees reach beyond the limits of their own experience and attitudes and begin to see that definitions are not givens in language itself, but are reflective of society's views, including issues of who in society wields the power.

Third, and finally, teachers have to be encouraged to cultivate a new attitude towards linguistics with regard to its perceived finiteness and absolutism. I no longer expect my teacher trainees to retain all the linguistics "facts" where they exist. My teaching of linguistics has evolved to the point where it is less and less knowledge-driven. Instead, trainees work with frameworks to construct their own understanding beyond what any linguistic theory can provide (Larsen-Freeman 1992). I am not talking about issues of making linguistic insights accessible; I am talking about altering the form of social participation through which teachers' understanding is constructed. In addition, I do believe trainees need to be socialized into the discourse of the linguistic community to the extent that they need to learn how to label linguistic structures according to conventional metalanguage. By being able to do this, trainees have abundant linguistic resources available to them.

I should make explicit another assumption underlying these three measures. Knowledge transmission as a vehicle does not work well. It is not only the form that linguistic theories are in that keeps them etic; it is also the way that participation with them is invited—or is not. If teacher educators lecture about linguistic theory and facts, the information may remain external as a reified body of information whose relevance is seen to have little bearing on the teachers' practice.

Thus what we are left with as language-teacher educators is the responsibility not to reject the contributions of linguistics outright, but rather to do a better job of not only researching teachers' knowledge bases, but also of helping teachers develop their own relationship to disciplines which might expand or contribute to this knowledge base.

Conclusion. In conclusion, it seems to me, as Stern has indicated, our attitude towards linguistics has undergone a very significant shift from "applying linguistics directly to treating linguistics as a resource to be drawn on for the benefit of pedagogy" (Stern 1983:4).

Thus clearly the role of linguistics in language teaching is more circumscribed than in the past. Rather than lamenting this fact, however, we should recognize linguistics for what it rightfully contributes—awareness of language and attitudes regarding language issues, and a source of insights which is indispensable as teachers construct their own understanding of teaching, learning, and language.

CONVERSATION

DIANE: I asked you to read this text because I had gotten the sense from our previous discussions that some of you would disagree with my position regarding the role of linguistics in language teacher education. While I call in the text for a new relationship to linguistics by language teachers, I do believe that it is essential that our students learn about linguistics so they can in turn help their students understand the nature of the target language and the learning challenges it presents. I teach a grammar-based applied linguistics course at SIT [School for International Training]. By the end of the course, I would like my students to have developed a way of looking at language. They should be able to pick up an authentic text and label the structures—to say something is a relative clause, for example. I feel that my students need to be able to identify the structures so they can draw on linguistic resources. They should also be able to identify the learning challenge—to say what is likely to be difficult about relative clauses for ESL/EFL students and to be able to identify a pedagogical strategy for how they would help students deal with the learning challenge. To learn to do these things, we examine different pieces of text, drawing on different schools of linguistic thought. We also look at ESL/EFL students' errors.

Although my course is less knowledge-driven than it used to be, it still seems to me that knowledge of the linguistic system is indispensable to language teachers. I have understood from some of your comments about a constructivist perspective that there is no place for decontextualized facts. And yet, in my role as gatekeeper, don't I have to ensure that my students have had as comprehensive an exposure to the structures of English as possible? And in order to achieve this goal, don't I have to draw up, if not a strict sequence, at least a checklist of English structures and issues about each that I want them to learn?

What Linguistic Knowledge Language Teachers Need and How They Learn It

JERRI: I think a discussion of why you teach grammar might be helpful. What helps them meet your goal? Often what we give students doesn't help them meet our goals at all. They can memorize what a relative clause is, and write it out, and yet never use it to really understand how languages work, in particular for their students. In fact, there may be a whole lot of interesting concepts and ideas about language that would be useful for them. For example, responding to students' writing when the students have a difficult time expressing a particular idea in English. What is it that a teacher needs to know to be able to respond in ways that are important, and what might you use to help do that? The answers to these questions may be very different from what they would be in a systematic presentation of someone else's discourse of what language is.

MAGGIE: In which case you have also addressed the gatekeeping question because you're not grading them on whether they know what a preposition is, or how a preposition functions, but on whether they can in fact recognize in their learners whether that is what's keeping them from being able to do whatever their task is and address it appropriately.

KATHLEEN: But don't they have to be able to name it?

MAGGIE: I wonder. There are probably many times that native speakers hear an error and can deal with it without being able to name it or explain to you why it's an error.

ELLEN: But when teachers see errors in second language data, they will need to know where they could go to get an explanation if they don't understand it. They would need to know what kinds of resources they could use.

SUZANNE: The issue of being able to identify something is an important one. You need to be able to label something so you can go and get information about it.

JERRI: That's the difference between naming it for the sake of naming it, and naming it for the purpose of getting help to figure out how to deal with it. I wouldn't expect students to come out being able to name everything there is to know, particularly in the beginning, but rather that they know enough to find out what they need to know.

DIANE: Right. Which is why I said my teaching is not as much knowledge-driven as it once was. I know from my own experience that students can cram all the grammatical minutiae for the purposes of an exam and then it's gone the next day. But I do insist that students learn how to identify something because it gives them access to other sources. And frankly, those sources will be very opaque unless they know some metalanguage and have a way to look at language. It's not simply a question of looking something up in a linguistic dictionary.

MAGGIE: Which is the reason we ought to say, "This is why you have to know the discourse of linguists and how they talk about things: the need to access information."

FRANCIS: When I see gatekeeping I always think about who is being filtered out. If you're assuming that you have to have this kind of disciplinary knowledge around linguistics or you won't get an M.A. through your program, then who is being deselected? And can you really demonstrate that they couldn't be good teachers? If you can't, then on what basis are you using that for gatekeeping purposes?

DIANE: We know that's a problem with gatekeeping. You could say that about anything. You don't need linguistics to be a good language teacher. You also don't need a methods course to be a good language teacher. You don't need to have an M.A. to be a good language teacher.

MAGGIE: Would we claim that a language teacher who has no understanding of the linguistic structure of the English language, no understanding of how the language works at all, could be a good ESL teacher?

KATHLEEN: What is your honest reaction if you hear a teacher say to you, "I don't know what an adverb is. I can't identify nouns and verbs in a sentence." Is that someone who should have a master's in teaching English as a second or foreign language?

DIANE AND OTHERS: No.

MAGGIE: All right. Everybody said no. Then as language teachers, why do they need to know the difference between a noun and a verb? Why is that an important thing for them to know?

ELLEN: Because the time will come when they will need to explain to their students the difference between nouns and verbs and the sorts of processes that nouns and verbs undergo. For example, my son's Spanish homework last night was to change some sentences from singular to plural. The nouns were easy, but when he came to the verbs, he wanted to just put a lot of *s*'s and *es*'s on them, too. So I started explaining to him about nouns and verbs. So how do you avoid that situation?

MAGGIE: What if someone could have explained to him what the difference is without using the words *nouns* and *verbs*—that one thing names a person, place, or thing, and the other is something that people or things do.

ELLEN: Those long phrases that explain that these are actions or these are things is why we have names like *nouns* or *verbs*. These words are just shorthand for the long phrases, and ultimately we'll come back to them. So why make it taboo to use the grammatical term?

MAGGIE: I keep coming back to the issue of gatekeeping. Let's assume that it isn't important that teachers have the kind of linguistics Diane is talking about. So she doesn't grade them or do any gatekeeping based on whether they know all the names and all the functions. Then what do you use for gatekeeping? What does somebody need to know? How can you tell if they know it?

JERRI: I would say it's exactly what Diane said in the first place. They can take texts, look at them, and try to figure out what's going on, what's working and what isn't, where they can go to get help. They may not be able to tell you a lot of details, but they will come to know them later when they're working with ESL students. Eventually, they may at some point say, "I'd like a really systematic view of this." That's different than putting people through a systematic view of how language works before they appreciate what they need and why they need it.

MAGGIE: So maybe it's the cart before the horse to teach it to them before they come to see that they need to know it?

JERRI: In some ways I think it goes backwards and forwards. Part of becoming interested in the structure of language occurs when a teacher realizes, "Yeah, I don't know how this works. I can't explain it to you. I need to go and find out whether someone has figured out a way to explain it." Not a fact, but a way.

DIANE: What do you mean by "not a fact"?

JERRI: Well when you mention a list, you always have to ask whose list? The description of the system that people are trying to figure out changes constantly. There are different ways of looking at the system, and teachers need to understand that these descriptions are just abstractions; they are not the language itself. These are ways to help teachers become interested in how language works, how meaning is made, and the consequences in one's everyday life. A good systematic review of a particular description comes after you've been looking at language for a long time. After you've played around with language for a while, you become interested in the language as a system. That comes later, not in the beginning.

DIANE: So, for you, knowledge of grammar is not a requisite for an M.A. You would not say a linguistics course is necessary for a fairly inexperienced teacher.

JERRI: Teachers need to play around with language, particularly in ways that make sense to them. Part of my job is to convince them that looking at language is fascinating and will be useful to them. One way to convince them is to create the contexts in which the information is obviously useful to them. So, for example, by having them tutor ESL students who ask them questions about the language that they can't answer, they will see the usefulness of these descriptions. I agree with the goals that Diane outlined for us at the start of our conversation. I, too, want the teachers to know how the language works and how to be able to explain it to second language learners. What I am questioning is the need for exhaustively and systematically working through a particular description of the language.

MAGGIE: So you're saying that teachers need to have this awareness of at least general categories and functions, even if they don't know all the discrete pieces within them. At least they would have a way to get in, to start to analyze and look, and to know where to go to get the information.

JERRI: There should be lists in the resources you're using, say the index in a textbook. A good index would not only name the item, it would give an example so you can find what you need to know. This is quite different from systematically going over the whole resource book step by step in a particular sequence. All I'm saying is that teachers don't have to memorize all the names and categories before they tackle the problems their students are having. They don't need to read everything in the resource book. If they know broadly how the language works, what issues might arise when ESL students use the language, and where you might locate some helpful ways of explaining the problem to the students, they'll eventually learn a great deal about the details of the language system.

MAGGIE: Given that, and the fact that, as Diane said, you can't expect to give them lists of language structures and functions and expect them to remember the structures and functions a year from now, how do you select what you teach them, given that you cannot anticipate which of it they are going to need when?

JERRI: I would use the context that I have available to me. For example, when teachers in different classrooms have been teaching thematic units, they can bring in the oral and written texts of their ESL students for the class to analyze. These texts become the basis for understanding particular language issues. Teachers can look for explanations that make sense to them. Some of the best resources for teachers aren't linguistic descriptions but pedagogical descriptions. They might look at a few descriptions and decide which ones make more sense to them.

MAGGIE: Then you're claiming that it doesn't matter if they know the difference between a noun and a verb. You might get cases where that issue doesn't come up, and your students get out without knowing it because you're not selecting specific crucial features that you think they need to know.

JERRI: Yes, but we use a variety of different texts, so eventually most issues are going to arise.

DIANE: But I don't think that is necessarily the case, so that's why you need a checklist. I can bring in a lot of texts but not all the structures are going to arise, not all the items on the list are going to be there, or they're not going to be there in all their functional diversity. So I might find an instance of the passive voice being used in one of the texts, but it might be limited to the passive voice being used when the agent is unknown. That's not the only time the passive voice is used. Its use in a text is a starting point for dealing with the passive voice, but I can't stop there.

Importance of Context

ELLEN: I also think we have to consider the teaching context itself, which is different for individual teachers. Their frames of reference are different with respect to the students they teach or think they are going to be teaching. Any particular individual's context for learning linguistics is going to be very different than the context of someone who works in a different setting, has different ideas about language teaching, and has a sense of different needs of their own students.

FRANCIS: That's true. Taking Donald [Freeman]'s perspective that we should take into account what teachers actually do before we construct our teacher education curricula [see chapter 5], maybe we need to look at and draw on what teachers actually do rather than on this disciplinary knowledge, which has been the traditional source. If you look at it from that point of view, what are the teachers who are actually delivering the ESL instruction doing? How much time do they need to focus on language, and how much time are they spending on other things? I remember observing a junior high school ESL teacher. One of the things that really struck me was how little time she spent on language analysis, on actually looking at the form itself. That was one percent, maybe, of her time.

SUZANNE: And another junior high or high school or college level ESL teacher might do nothing but focus on decontextualized forms. So how do you use that immense variety to make decisions about what you do?

MAGGIE: Well, it seems to me that there are two different questions. One is that of course you can't accommodate in the classroom each and every different context that each of your students is in outside that classroom. The other is that whether they want it or not may not be the thing that should drive how important a component we think it is in our classrooms or programs.

FRANCIS: I think there's a kind of arrogance to that. Maybe we should figure out what good teachers, successful teachers, are doing out there, and try to understand better what knowledge base they are drawing on. Then have that influence the way we do teacher education. Why should we just assume we know best?

DIANE: But just because you don't see it doesn't mean it's not operable. That's a purely performance-based view of teaching.

MAGGIE: Right, that's a really good point. Another one is who's going to decide who is a good and successful teacher? Some people would say the teachers who do the straight linguistic drills are good and successful and some would say they aren't. Somebody's got to make those judgments.

FRANCIS: I think that's where having a better grounding in what teachers do can be very helpful in making these choices. One of the jobs that I see teachers doing in public schools, since they are often more knowledgeable about language and about the way languages are learned, is that they have to transmit that knowledge to other teachers. So if they work in an ESL program, they might work with the mainstream teachers around the fact that this child is doing fine, actually, even though he's way behind in terms of language. He's going to catch up. Their professional job is not only working with students but also working with other teachers and administrators. So you might argue that even if you don't need this linguistic knowledge to work with first graders, you need it for another part of your job. That's why knowing more about what teachers actually spend their time doing is helpful in figuring out curriculum in teacher education.

DIANE: Are you saying that we should look at what they do because we may be wrong about what we think they need?

FRANCIS: Right. They may need this metalinguistic knowledge not because it's important for working with kids but because they need it in other parts of their job, like when they're interacting with parents. Or when they're interacting with another teacher, a teacher from whose classroom they pulled the child out, they may need a way of talking to that teacher about the child's progress.

DIANE: And if we happen to follow some teachers for a while and discover that they don't in fact use this linguistic knowledge, we don't see them using it, would that persuade you that they don't need it?

MAGGIE: I would have a lot of trouble taking what you can see teachers doing or saying as an indication of what framework they need in their heads. It may be that they don't directly talk about linguistics with the kids or the other teachers; it just doesn't come up as a topic. But that doesn't mean that the knowledge isn't necessary.

Knowing and Using

KATHLEEN: Could I take us another step? I think we've established that language teachers do need to know the terms used so they can have access to resources that will help them understand the language. My question concerns why a teacher needs to look up what a relative clause is. In a linguistics course, you're not just teaching them facts so they can go and look things up in a reference grammar. The challenge is what they do with that knowledge. They're not linguists, they're not grammarians, that's not the purpose of it. The purpose is to give them tools to be able to investigate the language. Why and how are they going to use the tools when they teach?

MAGGIE: Are you saying that the goal of the teacher education classroom then would be for them to explore why that's important to their practice and when they would need to use it?

KATHLEEN: Yes. That's a challenge for me. How to deal with that in the classroom.

SUZANNE: Awareness about language influences how teachers put the lessons together or what they have the kids do. A first-grade teacher, who doesn't need to use linguistics per se with her students, is using her awareness of language with them.

FRANCIS: But we know that linguistics isn't the only way to gain awareness of language. Poets may have no idea of linguistic theory but they have a profound knowledge of language.

SUZANNE: In a different way.

FRANCIS: Yes, but that knowledge could be used in teaching. I've seen people who are much more literary oriented, and have been trained in that tradition, who are great language teachers.

MAGGIE: That's sort of like asking if great mathematicians make great math teachers, or do they need to be trained in mathematics education? Is that the same question?

FRANCIS: I'm just thinking about it from the viewpoint of language awareness. There are a lot of different routes to language awareness. Linguistics is one of them and it's the way that our field has chosen to go, but it's not the only route to go.

JERRI: But wouldn't poets have a different kind of language awareness than people who studied linguistics?

MAGGIE: Yes, but I think Francis' point is whether that would make them any less good as language teachers.

KATHLEEN: That's my point. And I think it gets to that idea of what pedagogical content knowledge is [see chapter 5]. The fact that I know linguistics doesn't necessarily mean that it's going to help me as a teacher. So how do you create that bridge? In other words, do we have a clear idea of why people need this as teachers in their classrooms other than as understanding the language? To me that's the challenge of teaching a linguistics course. If you teach it as understanding the language, then it may or may not have an impact on teaching. You could teach it in a way that looks at what they are going to do with it in the classroom, but it still may not have an impact on what they actually do. You can have them analyze samples of ESL writing as a way of looking at the language. But I agree with Diane that there does need to be some systematicity. I have to have a road map of some kind so I don't get lost and they don't get lost.

FRANCIS: I was thinking about what you were saying, Diane, that if you just use authentic texts, you constrain yourself to that. Then one of the problems is that you might have one form of the passive, but you know that there's a much wider set of issues around passives. On the other hand, you always have a finite amount of time, and what any master's program teaches is only a fraction of the total knowledge that is available. So you always have to make choices. When you take them deeper into the passive, you've deselected spending time on speech events. How confident are you that it's more important to go into various possible uses of the passive as opposed to going into an element of sociolinguistics?

MAGGIE: Except that it's really a deeper choice that you're making. You can say, "Here are all the things that are out there that you could be aware of and might want to know the names of. I want to just give you a little sample of each and show you what's there." Or you could pick one area to go in depth to show the complexity of it, so they understand how deep and complex these things are. I think that's one of the central tensions of teaching. Do you do this surface covering of things or do you pick one and go in depth?

DIANE: Just as you ask your own students to pick the area that's going to be challenging for their ESL students, you pick the area where your students need the guidance, need the instruction. The choice of the passive over a speech event isn't necessarily because grammar is all there is to the language.

FRANCIS: That sounds faulty to me. I was just thinking about Ellen's example from her son. The reason they got into nouns and verbs was because of the assignment, not because of the language itself, but because the teacher set an assignment that required that kind of knowledge.

DIANE: I don't see that. Why do you say not because of the language itself? The language uses these endings.

MAGGIE: But the issue didn't come up because the kid had questions about the language that came from him.

DIANE: But he wouldn't because he didn't have the awareness. I presume that was the point of the lesson: to bring awareness. That is my job as a language teacher and as a teacher educator.

RESPONSE

Ellie Schmitt

I'm an ESL teacher at an elementary school in Madison, Wisconsin. I received my teacher training in elementary education, Grades 1 through 6, at the University of Wisconsin, Madison, and later received my ESL license through the graduate program there. The population with whom I work is primarily Hmong and Latino/Latina. My school has approximately 60 ESL students in kindergarten through fifth grade. The students' ability level varies from absolute beginners in English to fairly advanced. As I read this article on linguistics in teacher education, I considered whether linguistic training is necessary to teach the students that I teach, at the elementary level.

Throughout the discussion, I kept thinking that the need to know grammatical structures and rules depends on the individual classroom situation. I can imagine that an adult student, studying intensive English with the hope of attending a university, would need to be explicitly taught the rules of English. However, an elementary school student, who is just beginning to learn English, would be rather confused if the teacher started by teaching the structure of English using technical language and definitions. As with any sort of teaching, each classroom will be different and will require different teaching techniques.

At the elementary level, I rarely teach linguistic structures overtly. I often teach a grammatical concept in the context of a child's writing, for example, but I don't expect a child to memorize the names for the concept. I do, however, expect the child to be able to use that information in future writing samples. To help my students use these concepts successfully, I continually revisit and reteach them. When a child gets to an intermediate proficiency level, I use more specific linguistic language, but I still keep it relatively simple. I feel that it's important to start familiarizing the children with linguistic terms such as *noun, verb, adjective,* and so forth. These denote very basic linguistic concepts, and most likely the students will encounter words like these in their classrooms. Introducing them to such words will help them succeed in the regular classroom because the students will have some prior knowledge of the subject. I also teach the students some rules of language, such as how to make plurals. We practice when to use *-s, -es,* and how to know when the word is irregular and changes. I decide when to teach these concepts based on the students' own work. That way, students will find the concepts meaningful and relevant to their needs.

The notion of teaching these concepts brings me back to the discussion of whether ESL teachers need grammar-based linguistic training. I feel that ESL teachers need some training in linguistics. For ESL teachers at any level to adequately teach even the most basic grammatical concepts, they must have that knowledge themselves. For example, I wouldn't expect a car mechanic to tell me that something is wrong with my car just because it doesn't sound right when I start it. Similarly, I wouldn't want a teacher to tell a student that a sentence is wrong just because it sounds wrong. I'd expect the mechanic to know about the different parts of the car and what they do. I'd expect the teacher to know about the different parts of language and what they do. However, as I mentioned before, each classroom situation is unique. I can't imagine an elementary classroom teacher needing complex and obscure knowledge about grammar. It's important that the teacher know how to access that information if it's needed, but I don't feel that every ESL teacher should memorize it. It's simply not necessary or practical. The teacher should, however, have a good basic understanding of the English language's linguistic structure.

This discussion reminds me of my undergraduate training in elementary education and more specifically of my language arts classes. At that time, whole language was presented as the only "good way" to teach language arts. We were taught that whole language and phonics were two completely different approaches, and that you could use only one of them. The two could not be intertwined at all. In fact, I left feeling like only bad teachers would use phonics. Only after I had gained experience and further education did I realize that a good teacher could use both. In fact, I've come to believe that phonics can be useful in a whole language classroom.

In the same way, I believe that some direct instruction in grammar can be useful in an ESL classroom. Giving grammar drills day in and day out, however, is not good teaching. Grammar instruction is more appropriately used as an integral part of a successful ESL program, but it's important to remember that grammar instruction is only one aspect of such a program. Students have unique learning styles, so some children may benefit from grammar instruction. But good teaching requires a balance of approaches and teaching methods. Future ESL teachers should have a minimum basic training in grammar-based applied linguistics, but training programs should gear the training to the level at which the teacher will be teaching.

ACKNOWLEDGMENTS

The text section in this chapter is from D. Larsen-Freeman, "On the changing role of linguistics in the education of second-language teachers: Past, present, and future." In J. Alatis, C. Straehle, B. Gallenberger, and M. Ronkin (Eds.), *Georgetown University Round Table on Languages and Linguistics 1995* (pp. 722–723). Washington, DC: Georgetown University Press. Used with permission.

REFERENCES

Larsen-Freeman, D. (1983a). Second language acquisition: Getting the whole picture. In K. Bailey, M. Long, & S. Peck (Eds.), *Second language acquisition studies* (pp. 3–22). Rowley, MA: Newbury House.

Larsen-Freeman, D. (1983b). Training teachers or educating a teacher? In J. E. Alatis, H. H. Stern, & P. Strevens (Eds.), *Georgetown University Round Table on Languages and Linguistics 1983* (pp. 264–274). Washington, DC: Georgetown University Press.

Larsen-Freeman, D. (1992). Punctuation in teacher education. In J. Flowerdew, M. Brock, & S. Hsia (Eds.), *Perspectives on second language teacher education* (pp. 309–318). Hong Kong, SAR China: City Polytechnic of Hong Kong.

Larsen-Freeman, D. (1995). On the changing role of linguistics in the education of second-language teachers: Past, present, and future. In J. Alatis, C. Straehle, B. Gallenberger, & M. Ronkin (Eds.), *Georgetown University Round Table on Languages and Linguistics 1995* (pp. 722–723). Washington, DC: Georgetown University Press.

Stern, H. H. (1983). *Fundamental concepts of language teaching.* Oxford, England: Oxford University Press.

PROMOTING FURTHER CONVERSATIONS

Adger, C. T., Snow, C. E., & Christian, D. (2002). *What teachers need to know about language.* McHenry, IL: Delta Systems, & Washington, DC: Center for Applied Linguistics.

Cray, E. (2003). Knowing grammar for what it is: A critical approach to pedagogical grammar. In D. Liu & P. Master (Eds.), *Grammar teaching in teacher education* (pp. 11–24). Alexandria, VA: TESOL.

Savova, L. (2003). Grammar conversations: Educating teachers about grammar discourses. In D. Liu & P. Master (Eds.), *Grammar teaching in teacher education* (pp. 25–40). Alexandria, VA: TESOL.

Tyler, A., & Lardiere, D. (1996). Beyond consciousness raising: Re-examining the role of linguistics in language teacher education. In J. Alatis, C. Straehle, B. Gallenburger, & M. Ronkin (Eds.), *Proceedings of the 1996 Georgetown University Roundtable on Language and Linguistics* (pp. 270–287). Washington, DC: Georgetown University Press.

Widdowson, H. G. (1998). Context, community, and authentic language. *TESOL Quarterly, 32,* 705–716.

5

Examining Language Teachers' Teaching Knowledge

TEXT

Donald Freeman and Kathleen Graves

Donald: In an article published in the *TESOL Quarterly* (Freeman, 1989), I made the following statement:

> We [in language teacher education] have been proceeding in the wrong direction. Although applied linguistics, research in second language acquisition, and methodology all contribute to the knowledge on which language teaching is based, they are not, and must not be confused with, language teaching itself. They are, in fact, ancillary to it, and thus should not be the primary subject matter of language teacher education. (p. 29)

Kathleen: What then *is* the subject matter of language teacher education? Or, put another way, what is the knowledge base of teaching? In trying to answer that question, we've found it useful to make a distinction between the professional knowledge base of teaching, knowledge which defines people as teachers in the eyes of the community and of the profession, and the pedagogical knowledge base of teaching, that is, teachers' teaching knowledge, or what teachers know in order to do what they do. Although we're framing this as a dichotomy it is clear that they are related, and we want to pursue that relationship. So we posed another question: What do teachers know and how do they teach what they know? Our first response to that question was: Teachers *need to know* about the language, they need to know how to structure lessons, sequence material, how to teach the four skills of listening, speaking, reading, and writing, how to correct errors, and so forth. From a language teacher educator's standpoint, this list is a professional view of what needs to be covered, stemming from disciplines that have shaped second language teaching. The problem was that in responding with a list of "need to knows," we were being prescriptive rather than descriptive. We had changed the question from what teachers know to what they *need to* know; by inserting *need to* we had shifted to a prescriptive view. The issue in understanding the pedagogical knowledge base, or what teachers know in doing what they do, is a descriptive problem. If we jump to prescription, as we usually do, we miss the critical descriptive step.

Donald: This was the crux of the shift in our thinking: getting away from the idea of what teachers know as a list of discrete but interrelated topics which can be taught. What if teachers' teaching knowledge is really a process? At this point in the conversation we needed ways to rethink our understanding of teaching knowledge. Were there any useful constructs that could help us understand this shift?

The first construct we considered came from the work done by Lee Shulman and his colleagues in the Stanford Studies of Knowledge Growth in Teaching in the mid 1980s. They were working with the notion of subject matter knowledge and its relationship to what they termed pedagogical content knowledge. According to Shulman (1986):

> Pedagogical content knowledge . . . goes beyond knowledge of the subject matter per se to the dimension of subject matter knowledge *for teaching*. . . . Within the category of pedagogical content knowledge I include . . . the most useful forms of representations of those ideas, the most powerful analogies, illustrations, examples, explanations, and demonstrations—in a word, *ways of representing* and for-

mulating the subject that make it comprehensible *to others*. (p. 9, italics added)

Pedagogical content knowledge was an intriguing concept, not yet explicitly applied to language teaching. However, this construct was important to us because it affirmed that there was something unique about teachers' teaching knowledge that could be understood and described independently of disciplinary or professional knowledge.

Kathleen: It helped us to focus on the teaching act as a critical component for understanding the pedagogical knowledge base. It helped us to focus on the relationship between what a teacher knows about the subject matter and how a teacher helps learners to learn it. That for teachers, knowing the content *is* getting learners to produce it.

We have turned more recently to a second construct, instructional representations of subject matter knowledge, which is one of the offshoots of pedagogical content knowledge. We will call it *subject-matter representation* for short. Researchers at the National Center for Research on Teacher Learning, at Michigan State University (McDiarmid, Ball, & Anderson, 1989), have defined subject-matter representation as "a wide range of models that may convey something about the subject matter to the learner: activities, questions, examples and analogies, for instance" (p. iii). Thus, it is concerned with teachers' teaching knowledge in that it is about what teachers do with learners. Subject-matter representation lies at the intersection of several contextual forces: "Representations of subject matter are the products of weaving together the specific academic discipline involved with knowledge of learners, learning and the context" (p. iii). Further, how one weaves together these elements is shaped by one's beliefs and assumptions about each. Thus, when teacher educators teach certain representations, such as information gap exercises, they are presenting the results of a process of weaving together. The representations themselves are an outcome of a process of weaving together, but a contextualized outcome, not a replicable one. In other words, the representations that work well for one context may be inadequate in others.

Donald: For us, the important features of representations of subject matter were:

- The elements are integrated, they are "woven together." They involve both a process, the weaving, and an outcome, the representation.
- These representations are what learners of teaching need to work with, learn, and master in order to teach. But, while they can be learned as a repertoire, knowing when and how to use which particular form of representation cannot be learned as a repertoire because it is the context and the particular students that determine the appropriate representation.
- Classroom activities are surrogate forms of the discipline. The activities teachers have students do in class become the discipline for the students. For example, if a language teacher conducts a class in which students give cued responses about grammar, or has students memorize and repeat dialogues, or conducts question and response activities, these activities become what language is, even though they may contradict how we actually use a language in the world.
- Beliefs are critical: What teachers do in their teaching is shaped by what they believe. If the teacher believes on some level that learning involves rigorous practice, that belief will not be altered by introducing the concept of language as communication, since the teacher will continue to work in a way which emphasizes drill and practice of language forms and patterns.

Kathleen: What did we find useful about this concept? First, that teaching knowledge is contextual and relational. It takes us into the classroom and poses what teachers know in relationship to learners—that teachers' teaching knowledge is always in relation to learners. These are not generic learners, but particular learners in a particular context. As a learner of teaching there may be little you can learn through so-called generic situations, because they don't exist in the world. Second, it forces us to make the teacher a central figure, rather than the knowledge, since it is the teacher who must resolve all these considerations at once in the teaching. Third, it raises the issue: If teaching knowledge is about subject matter representation, and representation is the result of weaving together various understandings in the act of teaching, then how can we teach teaching knowledge?

CONVERSATION

Disciplinary Knowledge

KATHLEEN: At the end of the last conversation on linguistics and language teacher education [see chapter 4], I raised a question about the interface between teaching our students linguistic facts and helping them to understand how to teach them. That question connected with the difference between disciplinary knowledge and teaching knowledge that Donald and I discussed in our presentation at TESOL. Is that distinction somewhat problematic in our field? Because unlike history, for example, where part of what a history teacher might do is help learners understand how to be historians, I don't think that one of a language teacher's jobs is to help students become linguists. So I suggest we start first with whether we perceive a difference between disciplinary knowledge and teaching knowledge.

DIANE: Disciplinary knowledge would be the linguist's description of the language, for example?

ELLEN: In addition to the description of language, would it include one's theory of second language acquisition? Could that theory be based not only on the literature but also on one's personal experience?

DONALD: This is where it gets blurry in our field. In teacher cognition the actual framing of disciplinary knowledge is two things. It's the facts of the matter and it's how those facts get established. So in math it's what's true in math but also what it means to generate more information according to the paradigm of mathematical thinking. In biology it's how to think like a biologist, and it's also the facts of biology. How do you map that onto language? Is it linguistic knowledge and then second language acquisition?

JERRI: That's why disciplinary knowledge matters. What counts as linguistics depends on the theory of language you're working from. If you are working with Michael Agar's [1994] notion of languaculture, for example, language is more than linguistic structure.

DONALD: So therefore, we would say disciplinary knowledge doesn't include statements about how people learn the subject matter.

JERRI: I think we need to look at the issue with a different unit of analysis. Rather than the teacher or even the teacher-student as the unit of analysis, we should use the discourse community as the unit. For example, if you were studying physics and all you learned were the basic facts of physics, you would not be part of this discourse community of physics. But it's not easy to know the boundaries of a discourse community. Classroom discourse, for example, is shaped in part by a disciplinary community, a school discourse, a community discourse, and a state discourse, among others. And the way these different discourses are taken up within the particular community of the classroom is what we need to look at.

DONALD: We're not proposing that the unit of analysis is an individual.

JERRI: I'm saying I think we need to say more precisely what the unit of analysis is because in your argument the teacher is the central figure, and I think that's problematic.

KATHLEEN: How in your mind does this relate back to the idea of disciplinary knowledge?

JERRI: Because the community defines what the discipline is and what counts in the disciplinary community. What counts as disciplinary in the school community is something very different.

DONALD: But if you're sitting in a French 2 class, who is the one that's framing what French is?

JERRI: Classrooms are embedded in a variety of different institutions, all of which have an impact on what counts as French in the classroom. At U. Mass., for example, the exams, which are constructed at the department level, have great influence on what counts as French in the classroom. The nature of the exams is also influenced by a host of factors including the textbook companies, academic journals, the French Academy, the Haitian community, the list goes on. Even students, who may form communities resistant to French, influence what counts as French in the classroom. The teacher is not at the center in this configuration of influences.

DONALD: Everything you're saying makes good sense, but I think we pay far too little attention to how it is that teachers create the subject matter in the environment in which they work. That's not to say that they are central and they're the only people doing it, but there's far too little thought given to that act, and it's a political act; it's a cognitive act; it's all sorts of things.

JERRI: I don't disagree with anything you've said. I'm just saying that it needs to be taken further. You talk about teachers creating surrogate forms of disciplinary knowledge in their classrooms. But to understand these surrogate forms we need to look at the community in which the teacher is embedded, not merely the teacher's individual conception of that knowledge.

KATHLEEN: Maybe we can't answer the question "What is disciplinary knowledge?" because we can't pinpoint disciplinary knowledge. We may have differences of opinions or views on what disciplinary knowledge is.

Experiential and Conceptual Knowledge

DIANE: Can I try another angle? It seems to me that we could make a distinction between experiential knowledge and conceptual knowledge. I can come in with the experiential knowledge of the language that I'm going to teach because I'm a speaker of that language, but there's still value to having a conceptual knowledge of it.

DONALD: But what happens is that we often see people turning around and rehearsing that conceptual knowledge as if that's going to help learners get the experiential knowledge.

DIANE: For example, people who speak English come to a master's program and learn that what they've been doing all their lives is syntax and semantics, and they learn what the prescriptive and descriptive rules of the language are. Then they learn the conceptual framework, at least from a linguist's perspective. Now when they go to teach English, do they work from that conceptual knowledge by, for example, teaching a pronunciation contrast using a minimal pair drill? Or do they go back to simply using the language to teach it? They came in being able to use the language in the way that they wanted their students to, but were transformed through the education process of the teacher training program to see language in a different way. Having taken a phonology course they understand that what's important is meaningful distinctions in language. Therefore, they focus on a minimal pair phonemic contrast.

DONALD: I'm reminded of the first chapter of *A Way and Ways* where Earl [Stevick, 1980] has statements from teachers who talk about how they were better teachers before they became trained. They felt they connected more with learners and they really worked with what was going on.

DIANE: But as teacher trainers, we draw the opposite conclusion. We believe we are enhancing the experiential nature of our students' understanding by giving them conceptual frameworks.

KATHLEEN: Is it enough to teach our students these conceptual frameworks or is there something else in our programs that helps them to put the conceptual knowledge in the service of representing the subject matter?

DONALD: I think the subject matter representation experience is in a sense that participation in the community discourse. Maybe I'm putting words on Jerri's idea earlier. That's why someone who sits through a course taught in a particular way is taking in way more than the content, and that then becomes the way in which the subject matter is represented. There's another interesting question here, which is what the experiential knowledge is, if that's the term we're going to be using for *languaging* out there in the world. People know it when they see it, and they know it when they do it, and yet somehow that gets really changed by going through professional training. On the other hand, just walking in without it, you don't feel like you can be a teacher. So it seems that we have a paradox.

DIANE: So is it just finding a way to help teachers develop the conceptual knowledge that's not in opposition to, or does not undermine, the experiential nature of their own students' learning?

JERRI: Well, one of the problems with separating them is that even conceptual knowledge has to have an experiential base to it in some way. For example, when I first studied statistics by reading books, listening to lectures, and doing exercises, I passed the tests but had not acquired the concepts. Years later when I needed to use statistics to analyze data that I had collected, I did not draw on anything I learned in my earlier class. Instead I entered into an apprenticeship with my husband, who is a statistician. As I worked with my data, he would not only help me select the appropriate statistical method to analyze it, but he would also help me understand why. I remember thinking, "Wow! I'm finally beginning to understand the statistics." It was this experiential base with support that enabled me to acquire the concepts.

Learning to Teach

DIANE: I think what struck me most in Donald and Kathleen's dialogue was that the learning of teaching is a process and it doesn't matter what our models of language are, or whose they are, or what our models of classroom management are, or what our models of the kind of practices, activities, question-and-answer types are. If we treat any of those as static packages and impose them on a particular situation, it's not going to carry us far. We've got to see it as evolving.

DONALD: But that's pretty much of a commonplace, isn't it? Learning anything is a process, learning to swim . . .

KATHLEEN: Right, but look at swimming. The way people learn to swim is in the water with the coach there, but that's not how people learn to teach, except in the practicum part of it. Is the logical conclusion of this conversation that it should be like swimming? In other words, should the students be in the pool all the time?

DONALD: That's what professional development schools are about. There's another question, which is, to use the swimming metaphor, how do you start people out learning swimming in a way that's going to be the most productive? Given that it's a process, what's the best starting point? Maybe it doesn't matter. Maybe because it's a process you can start anywhere and there isn't a better or worse way. You've just got to start somehow.

ELLEN: If there is such a thing as doing it, then is there such a thing as teaching someone else how to do it? If what we really want is to produce good teachers who can do this, then we ought to try at least to find a way to identify what those things are.

JERRI: Maybe that's where the idea of teacher researcher comes in. Teachers continually learn content and teaching in the process of teaching rather than learning everything they need to know before they begin teaching.

DIANE: I think that's the nub of the problem. When a student comes out of a teacher training program and teaches language as disciplinary knowledge, as a conceptual model, the problem is that they have not gotten the fact that disciplinary knowledge was only a starting point.

KATHLEEN: But it's not really beside the point what the disciplinary knowledge is.

The Uniqueness of Language Teaching

MAGGIE: I don't think it's beside the point. One of the things I think about a lot is how incredibly different language teaching is from teaching another discipline. If I were in a science class, either teaching science or learning how to do science, there is a discipline, there is a base of knowledge that people can agree on. In order to count as a scientist you speak in very specific ways and about very specific things. I'm not sure that language is the same. I'm not sure that the field itself is as specific. Language is so representational of things. And there are so many other things embedded in it, and it's embedded in so many other things, that I do see teaching it as very different from teaching another discipline.

DONALD: I question whether language is that different from science or any other discipline. I think you know what a good speaker of a language sounds like if you're a good speaker of the language, just the way that, if you're a scientist, you can recognize another good scientist. If you're a speaker of French, you can recognize another good speaker of French.

MAGGIE: Yes, but as teachers, what we're trying to produce is a recognizable scientist or a recognizable speaker of French.

DONALD: So where's the difference?

MAGGIE: Because in science, it seems to me that there are relatively small communities that are coalesced around definitions and language and concepts of science, and actual knowledge that you can pass on, with terminology and ways of talking about it. I don't think language is that simple. To make someone a recognizable speaker of Spanish, what community, what Spanish, what worldviews does it represent? They may be able to speak the language in a clinical setting. Can they go somewhere and integrate into the community?

ELLEN: Is the goal that students be close to native speakers of a particular language? No. You just want them to be good speakers of the language, who can be understood, and who will be accepted by native speakers of that language. Can we expect after we educate them that they will know everything about the culture and fit right in? No. That's something that they have to do on their own.

DONALD: But to me that's not the compelling difference. The compelling difference is: Can I learn to be a scientist simply by going out and spending time in downtown Conway? If I don't speak English, I can spend time down there, and get something that begins to approximate that ability, the end point.

MAGGIE: You could learn science like that, by getting into the right community, if you had access to it.

DONALD: So then is the difference in our field and our disciplinary knowledge really that unfortunately we have a much bigger and easier-to-find community of people who do this thing than occurs with other subjects?

DIANE: That makes teachers look less essential. And if it makes teachers look less essential, it makes teacher educators look *really* less essential.

DONALD: Exactly.

ELLEN: That's like the examples teachers give of when people go to cocktail parties and they meet brain surgeons. They don't start giving them their opinions about how brain surgery ought to be done. But if they meet teachers, they give them their opinions, because everybody has been to school. And if they meet English teachers, if they're speakers of the English language, of course they know all they need to know, too.

DONALD: In a way you're saying that one of our major inferiority complexes is that we're burdened with two communities that are very easy to get into. One is teaching; because everybody's been a learner, a student in school, they think they know something about teaching. The other is being a speaker of English or of another language.

DIANE: Which is why you need conceptual knowledge, because we all are experiential knowledge acquirers and yet what distinguishes us is that we have this conceptual knowledge.

Apprenticeship Into the Discourse of Teaching

KATHLEEN: I think one of the things that we do in teacher education programs is give teachers a way of talking about teaching. A study done about the RSA-CTEFLA [Royal Society of Arts Certificate of Teaching English as a Foreign Language] showed that one of the things the teachers got was certain ways of talking about what they were doing. They could share in the community. We all know this about discourse communities. I think that what a good teacher preparation program does is give teachers ways of looking at and talking about what they're doing. That's one of the things they need in order to be able to become self-directed teachers. I think that each of our programs probably gives the teachers we teach different ways of talking about their teaching. Is it necessary that they use the same words or even the same ways of seeing? Or is it simply the fact that we have a coherent view that they coconstruct with us that then enables them to see things, to make decisions, and to be good teachers? Even though the talk they talk at SIT may be different from the talk they talk at U. Mass., they go into their classrooms being able to talk that talk.

MAGGIE: Kathleen is saying that part of what we're doing is giving people a language with which they can talk about teaching together. But it also gives them tools to know what to look at, how to look, where to begin to look. The more languages and words and ways they have, the deeper they can look.

KATHLEEN: If I were to envision something for the future, it would be that our students not come and take classes where we are but that we have bands of students who spend a year in Mexico or other places where we provide internships, and Diane and I go there and do seminars with them based on what happens in their communities.

MAGGIE: That's much closer to an apprenticeship model. They're doing it, they're apprenticing.

DONALD: But the apprenticeship model is there anyway. That's what teacher socialization is. You're learning how to do it from the people who are already doing it. That's the apprenticeship model.

MAGGIE: Except that pulling them into the university and giving them the classes first and then sticking them out there is not as much an apprenticeship model as going on-site where they are.

Responsibility and Agency

ELLEN: I want to go back and ask a devil's advocate kind of a question. Supposing I'm a young, aspiring ESL teacher, and I want to go to the best place to be trained so I go to SIT. I want to know what it is that I'm going to gain or get from being at SIT that's going to make me a good teacher. That question is underlying this conversation in a way that's bothering me because if there is such a thing as good teaching, do we know what it is, can we identify it, can we teach it, aren't we responsible for teaching it?

DONALD: I think there's a deeper thing that you're going to get out of it, a thing I wouldn't tell you if you asked me what you're going to get out of it. One of the givens in the language of our program, probably the central given, is that the only unacceptable explanation for why something didn't work in a lesson is, "It was my student's fault." It's not that people say that's unacceptable, it's just that they won't hear it. That is silenced as a way of talking. You learn not to say it, so after a year you're socialized into realizing that the only way I can't diagnose what's not working in my teaching is by saying, "those dumb students."

ELLEN: Therefore, because I'm always responsible, I will always be searching for what I can do better.

DONALD: Right, and there's a certain dysfunctionality with it because then you go into a situation where you have a ton of problems.

JERRI: It's asking the teacher to take all of the blame for what's going wrong. I think that's problematic when in fact the responsibility must be distributed across the society.

DONALD: What about the notion that focusing on yourself as a teacher has both responsibility and agency as part of it? We want to capture the agency side without overdoing the responsibility side because it is not accurate to say you're responsible for everything. Nor is it accurate to say you can do something about everything. Going back to this idea of launching, we can try to launch a sense of agency in the individual. This is why you like the first-year teacher, because you know that she's going to be up until four in the morning doing lesson plans, and even if they're not the greatest lessons in the world, there will be charisma behind them because she certainly wants them to be good. That's the agency side of it. I can do something. So how do you keep that sense of agency alive? I think that's what the supervision does. In the program Kathleen and I directed in Brazil, there was no direct supervision by faculty. It was cosupervision of teachers talking with each other, and they managed to keep the sense of agency alive. Going back to your question, Ellen, about what you're taking from the program. You will leave this program with a sense of your ability to do something. And the question is: Can you learn that agency without at least embarking on a certain amount of responsibility? They're pretty hard to separate.

RESPONSE

Amy Powell Faeskorn

Thank you for asking me to respond to this LTEC discussion. Disciplinary and teaching knowledge and the role of teacher education in imparting them are quite fascinating and difficult to resolve. Six months after completing a master's program at the School for International Training, which changed me in so many important ways, I find myself wondering what role, if any, the language teacher education I received has played in improving my actual teaching practice. Clearly, I have emerged with a greater grasp of both types of knowledge as well as an enhanced ability to articulate my beliefs about teaching and learning, which were greatly altered by the kind of reflective practice my professors compelled me to undertake. I certainly consider myself to be more of a trained professional now. But am I a better teacher in any measurable or noticeable way?

As I reflect on myself as a teacher both before and after completing a graduate program, I find that disciplinary and teaching knowledge have left many traces. I decided to obtain a master's degree largely because I wanted to improve both my disciplinary and teaching knowledge. After teaching English overseas for 2 years, I felt that I had a fairly solid grasp of disciplinary knowledge. Though I had received some initial training, which culminated in a TEFL certificate, I came to know and understand the English language as subject matter experientially. As a beginning teacher, I was often confronted with having to teach an unfamiliar grammatical structure. I would study it until I felt confident enough to teach it. Trained in the communicative approach, I used student-centered teaching. Yet I found that, over time, I was growing increasingly dissatisfied with the quality of my teaching, and I was beginning to doubt myself and my abilities. On an intuitive level, I still believed I was a good teacher, but I was plagued by a feeling that my practice lacked something essential.

I realize now that what I most took away from my graduate program was an altered perception of myself as a teacher. Although the program provided me with vital disciplinary and teaching knowledge—a broader understanding of linguistics, second language acquisition, the cognition of teaching and learning, and course development, for example—it was the process of unearthing my beliefs about language teaching and learning, examining them carefully and critically, having them changed or reinforced as a result of being exposed to new ideas, and ultimately rearticulating and defending them that allowed me to forge an identity as a teacher.

The issue that enables me to connect my experience in the program most directly with the content of your discussion is community in teacher education. I agree with Donald when he says that "one of our major inferiority complexes is that we're burdened with two communities that are very easy to get into. One is teaching; because everybody's been a learner, a student in school, they think they know something about teaching. The other is being a speaker of English or another language" (this volume, pp. 98–99). Clearly, issues unique to language teaching create a kind of existential crisis for language teacher educators that professional developers in other fields do not face. I am reminded here of the corollary "teaching does not cause learning," which takes on particular significance for language teachers, whose role, it can be argued, is largely nonessential given that the subject matter can be and often is learned without formal instruction. However, as you point out, language teacher education programs provide teachers with "a way of talking about teaching." The ongoing interactions and discussions I maintained with peers represented a crucial component of my experience in the M.A. in Teaching (MAT) program.

I find Donald's distinction between responsibility and agency particularly useful for framing the goals of language teacher education. The MAT program taught me to shift the responsibility onto myself and my teaching when appropriate, and it showed me how I can contribute to the field of language teaching, whatever the context or scale may be. Looking back, much of the frustration I experienced as a new teacher stemmed from a misguided understanding of my role as a teacher, both in and out of the classroom. I now believe that good teaching extends beyond sound classroom practice; it demands an ethic of community service and commitment to progress, both individual and collective. By its very nature, teaching is agency for change, and language teaching is even more so. Thus, successful language teacher educators are those who encourage teachers to strike a balance between responsibility and agency while at the same time talking the talk at all levels of their own involvement in the program, be it internship supervision, curriculum design and delivery, or advising.

Thank you again for allowing me to comment on this issue. It is precisely this sort of endeavor—examining myself critically and honestly in a particular context of teaching and learning—that I have come to value so much through my experience as a graduate student in the MAT program. In a sense, disciplinary knowledge has taken on a double meaning for me. It involves my familiarity with and ongoing learning of the subject matter I teach and a willingness to discipline myself into participating in regular activities of reflection and self-examination such as this one. In doing so, I feel that I am becoming a good teacher.

ACKNOWLEDGMENTS

The Text section in this chapter is excerpted from D. Freeman and K. Graves, *Reexamining language teachers' teaching knowledge: A conversation.* Paper presented at the 27th Annual TESOL Convention and Exhibit, April 1993, Atlanta, Georgia.

REFERENCES

Agar, M. (1994). *Language shock: Understanding the culture of conversation.* New York: William Morrow.

Freeman, D. (1989). Teacher training, development, and decision making: A model of teaching and related strategies for language teacher education. *TESOL Quarterly, 23,* 27–46.

Freeman, D., & Graves, K. (1993, April). *Reexamining language teachers' teaching knowledge: A conversation.* Paper presented at the 27th Annual TESOL Convention, Atlanta, GA.

McDiarmid, G. W., Ball, D. L., & Anderson, C. W. (1989). *Why staying one chapter ahead doesn't really work: Subject-specific pedagogy* (NCRTE Issue Paper 88–6). East Lansing: Michigan State University.

Shulman, L. (1986). Those who understand: Knowledge growth in teaching. *Educational Researcher, 15*(2), 4–14.

Stevick, E. (1980). *Teaching languages: A way and ways.* Rowley, MA: Newbury House.

PROMOTING FURTHER CONVERSATIONS

Ball, D. L. (2000). Bridging practices: Intertwining content and pedagogy in teaching and learning to teach. *Journal of Teacher Education, 51,* 241–247.

Freeman, D. (1994). Knowing into doing: Teacher education and the problem of transfer. In D. C. S. Li, D. Mahoney, & J. C. Richards (Eds.), *Exploring second language teacher development* (pp. 1–20). Hong Kong, SAR China: City Polytechnic of Hong Kong.

Grossman, P. (1990). *The making of a teacher.* New York: Teachers College Press.

Shulman, L. (1987). Knowledge-base and teaching: Foundations of the new reform. *Harvard Educational Review, 57*(1), 1–22.

Tsui, A. (2003). *Expertise in teaching.* New York: Cambridge University Press.

6

The Role of Research in Language Teacher Education

TEXT

Margaret (Maggie) Hawkins

I've been struggling with the notion of research recently because my career seems to be moving in that direction. I started as a classroom teacher, passed through consultant, program developer, and teacher educator, and now, although I will still fulfill all those roles, I will be focusing on research. While I always saw research as informing my work, I never, until now, saw research as my work.

I just found an article by Mary Kennedy (1997) in which she provides a historical overview of educational research, in the interest of exploring why research has had so little effect on practice. She identifies four major critiques of educational research:

1. "The research itself is not sufficiently persuasive or authoritative. . . . [It doesn't] provide compelling, unambiguous, or authoritative results to practitioners."

2. "The research has not been relevant to practice. It has not been sufficiently practical, it has not addressed teachers' questions, nor has it adequately acknowledged their constraints."

3. "Ideas from research have not been accessible to teachers."
4. "The education system itself is intractable and unable to change, or it is conversely inherently unstable, overly susceptible to fads, and consequently unable to engage in systematic change." (p. 4)

Among other claims, Kennedy points to the impossibility of research providing definitive answers because classrooms are local environments, with differing components and influences, and the social contexts (both within and without) are continually changing (as is language itself, I would add). She feels that meaningful research (building on Brown, 1992) has to "occur within the natural constraints of real classrooms and must accommodate as best it can the multiple confounding influences that are there" (Kennedy, p. 5).

My doctoral research was an ethnographic study of a particular graduate-level second language acquisition class that was part of an ESL and bilingual teacher education program. The course and participant structure were unusual: The instructor (Jerri Willett) tried to incorporate and enact constructivist theory. Part of the work I was doing centered on one student in a collaborative group. Despite the extensive work done to ensure that all group members had a participatory, authoritative voice, the group marginalized this student because his experiences and ways of behaving, communicating, and interacting were outside academic norms (even though the group's explicit task was to analyze culturally diverse experiences, behaviors, and so forth). The study as a whole provided evidence for the claim that even with the best of intentions, and with alternative designs and structures, it is difficult to overcome ingrained traditional modes of schooling, including how (and by what) participants are positioned within systems.

So what? Of what value is this to me or others? And given the critiques Kennedy identifies, what difference can it possibly make? Well, I think it's both compelling and authoritative because I purposely constructed, conducted, and displayed my work in ways that resonate within other discourses. I appealed to an audience (or audiences) from whom I wanted validity and professional respect, a scholarly audience with certain intellectual interests in common. Does positioning my work in this way mean that it's not accessible to teachers? I hope not. Do I feel that it has anything to offer teachers and practitioners? Absolutely.

Because I have entered, in various ways, conversations about such issues as power relations, identity, positioning, status, cultural differences, and empowerment, I have come to hold a very strong set of beliefs about equity and social justice. I feel my work illustrates issues that every teacher ought to worry about: how power relations get enacted in academic classrooms, and how students come to be positioned as either insiders or outsiders. I consciously tried not to slip too much into the sorts of elite discourses that exclude those who aren't inside them. Is my research unambiguous? No. It seems to me that because we're dealing with practice, including teachers' local conditions, questions, and constraints, the claims are neither clear-cut nor completely generalizable. But this doesn't render the research non-authoritative, irrelevant, inaccessible, or impractical. What does this type of research do?

Well, for me, it raises my awareness of how power relations are discursively constructed turn by turn in conversation. This has deepened my reflection on my own classroom practices and heightened my awareness of interaction. I can purposefully plan interventions and strategies and thus promote a more equitable (and political) atmosphere. It also satisfies one of my deepest goals: I am making a contribution to the issues that engage me most. I feel that, through my work, others might explore these issues in their own practices or at least stop and reflect on how the tacit, taken-for-granted practices and pedagogies position their learners. And this addresses Kennedy's (1997) fourth point: Can the educational institution change? I don't know. But I believe individuals can, and the best way to encourage the process is by raising issues, challenging deep-seated beliefs and practices, and promoting reflection. I believe with all my heart that social change is necessary and hope that I am contributing to the process.

So I'd like to explore everyone's relationship (professionally and/or personally) with empirical research: to explore what the role of research is in our field, and in our lives.

CONVERSATION

FRANCIS: I was really struck with Kennedy's ideas in today's text. She identifies four major critiques of educational research. Number one is that the research itself doesn't provide compelling, unambiguous, or authoritative results to practitioners. Much of educational research is qualitative, and qualitative research is open-ended. There are multiple interpretations. The kind of research we're oriented toward is very thick descriptions of classrooms. Teachers must wonder, "How does this generalize to my case?" So I wonder if that open-endedness isn't one of the things that makes research very difficult for teachers to relate to.

JERRI: Yes, and also the fact that you never have it right. When do you stop? You end when the money and time run out. Another thing is how you represent what you've done. You can say, "I was the researcher and I'm the authority here" versus "Here are our interpretations and stories. And here are the things we don't know, but these are some of the implications."

FRANCIS: I wonder if putting in the limitations of the research undermines your authority. That's what Kennedy is saying. Practitioners start reading a research article and say, "Why would I want to read this? This person doesn't even have anything definitive to tell me." When we truthfully represent the reality of the research, which is that it is always incomplete, that seems to turn people off to it.

JERRI: That goes back to the way knowledge is oriented in our education system. Most of us, including the teachers we work with, have gone through years with objective, multiple-choice tests. How else would we look at knowledge?

FRANCIS: One way that this kind of thinking could inform teacher education is if we can decenter knowledge and problematize it in some way. I think that's clearly one of the things that's happening in Jerri's program. [See chapter 1.] It challenges some of those basic assumptions about the nature of knowledge and authority, and it's very disquieting for some people, but it's very exciting for others.

What Is Research? What Kind of Research Is Relevant?

MAGGIE: I'd like to back up a little and see if we can agree on what research is. At a TESOL session on research that I attended a couple of years ago, people put out the idea that basically any act of inquiry counts as research, so any time teachers pose questions about their practices and try to find answers, that's research. That was one end of the continuum. Then somebody else stood up and argued that research has to be quantitative and rigorous. Otherwise, what good is it?

FRANCIS: That's interesting. I've been associated with the American Educational Research Association since 1988, and in that time I've seen a tremendous shift in how research is viewed. There is now a more open stance toward all kinds of research and toward accepting qualitative research as legitimate.

SUZANNE: The quantitative-qualitative debate has been with us for many years, and most people will admit that we need both. But there's another issue now that we've got teachers doing research. Do you evaluate their research according to the same criteria that you use to evaluate university research? I just reviewed an article for *TESL-EJ* that described a teacher research project. It was a very good example of teacher research, but if we used our normal criteria for publishing in *TESL-EJ*, it wouldn't make it.

JERRI: I don't think that teacher research has the same kind of infrastructure that exists for other kinds of research. Sometimes those research procedures keep you from seeing things. Why should university research dictate what we do in teacher research? I think that's a reasonable question to ask, but I don't think you can throw everything out. You must have some accountability for your interpretations.

MAGGIE: One of the things that interests me is what sort of research counts. What is the nature of our field, and what sorts of research inform us about the things we need to know as teacher educators or that language teachers might need to know? It seems to me that almost all research is relevant to what I do, and that opens up incredible possibilities. What isn't relevant?

FRANCIS: The research that I think of as being less relevant, or at least less interesting to me, is experimental research, because in education it's essential to capture the contextual variables.

MAGGIE: So you're saying that any time you isolate a specific feature and take it out of its own context, it becomes much less helpful because it's decontextualized. It doesn't show all the multiple nuances and influences that go on in an actual classroom.

FRANCIS: Yes. I'm not saying that quantitative research couldn't be helpful, but I find experimental research to be much less compelling in the field of education.

SUZANNE: I agree totally. As soon as you try to do experimental things to get somebody to learn something, you're distorting the natural learning context and you're not going to get the same kinds of results that you would see in real educational settings.

ELLEN: I agree with you about experimental research, but I think it can sometimes suggest questions that are worth looking at from a different perspective.

JERRI: The irony is that experimental researchers would say that's the role of ethnography. They would say that qualitative research can't tell you what causes something but experimental research can. What qualitative research does is tell you the kinds of interesting questions you could explore. There's an interesting twist there.

SUZANNE: Another point experimental researchers would make is that you can't generalize qualitative research beyond the context in which it was done.

MAGGIE: Exactly. And therefore can you make any valid claims? That's one point Kennedy discussed in her article. What is educational research, and where does it come from? Her conclusion was that although we don't have all the answers, we've come a great distance in realizing that classrooms are very complex ecologies. You can't take something out of context and isolate it and think you've come up with anything valid. But when you look at something with all its contextual variables, you can't generalize it. How does this inform somebody else in a completely different context with completely different variables?

FRANCIS: One of my students at SIT wrote a thesis called "Exploring the Teacher/Researcher Communication Gap" [Caulk, 1996]. He went to a summer TESOL institute and had practicing teachers and researchers read a teacher-oriented article and a research article on roughly the same topic. He then interviewed them about the reactions they had. The kinds of reactions that teachers had to research were quite interesting. Can I read one little piece here? This is a teacher talking about the research article:

> I think a researcher can get so excited about a subject that they want to find out all of the really nitty-gritty, fine-tuned things about it. They forget that sometimes the audience doesn't really care that much. I think that one instructor or one researcher wants to impress another one with all those quotes and how smart they are and all these articles that they've read and how they can incorporate this and come up with new ideas, and then they have to prove these points because they know if they don't prove these points with lots of quotes then one of their other professional friends is going to take this article and start shooting it full of holes.

JERRI: When you think about our educational system and the way we've approached knowledge in schools, it's not surprising that teachers have that kind of perspective on research. I'm sure there are cases where they're right. There are some people who are just trying to impress; that's part of the game. Even the idea that researchers are going crazy over these little details is true, but that's because of their level of knowledge about the subject. I would be bored by someone else's details, too, if I weren't interested in that subject. Students rarely get to understand why details in research are important. They're usually tested on random facts that the teacher wants them to know, so they memorize the facts, which don't mean anything. Promoting inquiry isn't as common as we like to think it is. So it's not surprising that teachers, who are the purveyors of knowledge that comes out this way, would have that view of research.

SUZANNE: If research in education should inform what teachers do, then the teachers are the audience for the research that other people do. So how can we get around this problematic aspect of it?

JERRI: Well, if teachers aren't doing research themselves, I don't think research really informs what they're doing. It's when they're doing research that it informs their practice.

Teacher-Researcher Relationships

SUZANNE: When the action research movement started, I had high hopes for it. Teachers certainly ask questions and try to find answers to them all the time, which is inquiry. But I'm seeing more and more of a dichotomy between teacher research and researcher research. I was hoping that the two would come together more, but I don't see that happening.

JERRI: It's very hard to look at your own practice. Researchers are usually looking at someone else's practice. When you're looking at your own practice, it's very difficult to see those things that go against your beliefs. The hardest thing I've found in working with teacher researchers is that when they find things in their own teaching that don't go with their beliefs or with their images of themselves as teachers, they equate it with bad teaching. But they're not going to answer their questions if they're only looking at the things that they think are all right and use that to validate who they are as teachers.

This kind of work needs to be done with an audience because they don't see it if they don't have feedback from others.

SUZANNE: That reminds me of a particular concern I have that arose from the observations I did for my TeacherSource book [Irujo, 1998], when I spent a semester observing a second-grade bilingual classroom. The teacher was delighted to have me there. I think she saw herself as a model, although I told her that I was trying to present the reality of an ordinary bilingual classroom. She loved the first parts of the book that she read. She thought I had captured her perfectly. Of course, I wrote the easier parts first. When she read the whole thing she was very disappointed with parts of it. She asked me if I was trying to show people what they shouldn't do. So we went over it again, and I tried to get her to understand that there was no evaluation there. I was trying to be very objective and not evaluate things. But of course there was evaluation. I sent her the final manuscript, but I haven't heard from her since. So for me, the relationship of outside researcher and classroom teacher is an issue.

JERRI: I wrote something for today's meeting that resonates with that very much.

I've often asked myself the same kinds of questions that Maggie has raised in her text. While I certainly enjoy receiving validation and respect from the scholarly community, I'm personally drawn to the intellectual challenges and sense of discovery that come from doing research and finding or creating a story. I have become concerned about how little teachers are involved in research. In fact, they're often positioned negatively. My experience with one teacher illustrates the extent of the problem. I believe this was one of the most talented teachers I had ever known, and yet my being a researcher and her being the teacher was problematic. Eventually she came to see what I was researching as helpful to her. I was troubled by my realization that researchers were considered enemies by teachers. Now that I have been the teacher in several research projects, however, I'm beginning to understand their sentiments. It isn't being positioned negatively that's the problem, so much as the thinness of the stories often told. It just doesn't capture what you know or can see and the things you've seen in the classroom. Now that I'm doing collaborative research with the teacher [see chapter 2], some of these problems have resolved themselves. We are engaged in all aspects of research and that includes data collection, analysis, and writing.

With the collaborative research you don't get in the situation that Suzanne was in and that I was in with my teacher. I respected her very much and I thought she was fabulous, and I couldn't understand what the problem was.

MAGGIE: So it's the interpersonal relationships.

JERRI: Yes. I also think you create a better story. You get more nuances and richer kinds of texts in ways that neither a teacher nor a researcher could do on her own. I'm not elevating teachers here, because they tell thin stories as well. They tell very narrow stories with a whole lot going on that they don't see. I'm not saying that collaborative research is the answer to everything because it's hard work. There's no space, there's no time, and it doesn't always work out.

FRANCIS: The theme of the alienating effect of research resonates with my own experience. As a doctoral student I started doing some research in a high school classroom. I was unable to complete it because the teacher became uncomfortable with me doing research there, and I was tossed out. This woman is still furious with me, and that was a long time ago. So I found out how difficult it can be working with somebody else and for them to be the object of the research inquiry. It seems to be very painful for people. The kind of research that I'm involved with now is collaborative research with an ESL teacher. I've been extremely careful to make it collaborative, to try to let questions come from him. I've moved very slowly with this research because I'm so afraid that somehow it's going to go awry again. So for me, one of the important issues is the problematic nature of research, particularly around the relationship between the researcher and the researched.

SUZANNE: Does it have something to do with opening up your own practice to scrutiny? With the teacher I observed, I started out by inviting her to sit down with me for a few minutes after school and talk about what I was seeing. She had no interest at all in doing that. So we talked only during semistructured interviews in which I explored some of her views. We never actually just sat down and shared ideas about what I was seeing in her classroom. We never talked about my perceptions versus her perceptions.

JERRI: When you think about it, what is the investment in doing that for someone for whom things work?

SUZANNE: One of the reasons she was very willing to have me come in was that she was very confident about what she was doing.

FRANCIS: Okay, so at a certain point she read your description of what was happening and probably for the first time had someone characterize her practice from an outside perspective. That wasn't a very happy moment for her. Something about that was upsetting, and you haven't been able to find out any more than that. She didn't write you at any point?

SUZANNE: No. I was feeding her things as I wrote them. I had written up the things that seemed to work well first because they were the easiest, and she was delighted. She told me, "You captured me." Then I showed her the piece that changed her mind, which was where I followed three children through a whole day. I looked at it again after she reacted so negatively, and there was some evaluative language at the end about how little academic work the kids had actually done during the day.

FRANCIS: But in your opinion that was an empirical statement.

SUZANNE: Yes, but I didn't have to say those were the only things these children did. I could have just said that was what the children did today. So I went back and changed that language to try to make it more objective. But the next time I saw the teacher she said, "What are you trying to do? Are you trying to show that I'm not teaching these kids? Are you trying to show that I'm a bad teacher?" I said, "No, I'm trying to present the reality of an urban second-grade bilingual classroom. I want other teachers to think about what these children are doing all day. Are there ways it could be done differently?"

MAGGIE: I have a problem assuming that anybody could write an account of a classroom that's objective. The very decisions about what it is you would report or talk about or notice or not notice would make you biased. When things happen in real time and the teacher has to rely on her memory of what her perceptions were at the time, that allows her to be much more selective and therefore biased.

JERRI: Theoretically, it seems to me what you have now is just one story of that classroom. She has another story. In a joint narrative, you would talk and try to understand one another's stories. In a joint narrative, you could take into account all of these issues including who your audience is and how you are going to look at the data. You could also frame things in a way that isn't damaging to people who are there but at the same time come to the agreement that we're not going to try to smooth out rough edges. These are the kinds of things that can be negotiated.

FRANCIS: One of the things that I'm hearing is that from Suzanne's experience with the teacher, she wasn't thinking of this as a way to work on her practice. The book would capture her model practice. And it sounds like Suzanne came in with the idea of capturing what was happening and then writing it up. The teacher was confident that her practice was solid so that if Suzanne did a good job of capturing it, things would go well. That seems like such a different orientation than inquiry, where you are just looking for interesting questions and issues to explore that would stretch practice.

SUZANNE: You know, looking back on it now, there are a lot of things I would have done differently. But if I had gone in presenting this as joint inquiry I think I probably would have gotten too involved in it to be able to do even a semiobjective presentation of the practice that was going on in that classroom. I'm not sure that approaching it as joint inquiry would have worked for my purposes. It would have been a chronicle of joint reflection of what was going on in this classroom rather than a verbal snapshot of the classroom.

MAGGIE: So that's different than what Jerri's doing, which is a collaborative discovery between teacher and researcher over a long period of time, where you start out in a spirit of inquiry and you see what develops. If articles and books come, they do, but the point is to engage in the research itself collaboratively. A teacher doing this kind of joint inquiry has a different voice than the teacher Suzanne worked with, who was being written about or feeling evaluated, as she maybe did in this case.

JERRI: Which is why we need the agreement between researchers and practitioners that we're doing this together.

MAGGIE: But it's not just doing it together. It's really looking at the nature of a relationship. That's one of the reasons I buy so fully into the notion of professional development schools, in which you have a core of people who work together over an extended period of time. You develop the trust and the relationships with the people and the whole collaborative nature of the enterprise over time.

RESPONSE

Jo-Anne Wilson Keenan

Thank you for inviting me to listen in on your conversation about research. I found it interesting because I have been thinking lately about so many of the questions and issues that you raise.

I have been teaching in the public schools for 30 years, and even in the beginning of my career I was not satisfied with the approaches to teaching and learning that were available to me. I started searching then, and I'm still searching, for more effective approaches. My inquiries eventually led to my doctoral work, in which I studied the writing of urban first-grade students and described ways in which teachers could build upon students' knowledge of written language. Since that time, I have been engaged in a 10-year collaborative research project with Jerri and a colleague of hers. (For one of the products of that research, see Wilson-Keenan, Willett, & Solsken, 1993.) We are looking at what happens when urban families become curriculum partners in my primary multiage classroom. As the school-based teacher researcher on this team, I helped develop strategies for family participation in language arts instruction and conducted ethnographic research on language practices during family visits in the classroom. Research in general, and teacher research in particular, is very important to me.

While the research project was going on in my classroom, we met every other week. Sometimes I felt vulnerable. At one point, four different researchers had come into my classroom during a single week, each one interested in discussing a different issue. I was overwhelmed. To get all of it back under control, I wanted to isolate them to one part of the week. But no sooner had I said that than I realized that the visits were part of the fabric of the classroom community. It was not possible to turn back at this point because I was not willing to give up. After those meetings I would go home and think about the questions that had been raised about my practice. If things were really bothering me, I'd call or e-mail Jerri or her colleague to talk more about it. Usually we would clarify things, and I began to make small and then larger changes in my practice. I often found that when issues about practice were raised in the meeting, I needed time to think about them. I was not always able to analyze situations on the spot. Often my initial reaction had to play itself out first.

I also found that sometimes the smallest issues were the tips of the largest icebergs. For example, I was in the practice of addressing the children as *boys and girls*. At one of the meetings someone suggested that by addressing the children in this way, I was defining two distinct groups in the classroom. My first reaction was, well of course I say, "Boys and girls, it's time to . . .". That's the way teachers talk. I couldn't see what all the fuss was about. But I kept thinking about it and realized that not only was I naming the separate groups, I was always putting the boys first. So I began trying out other ways of addressing them. I tried *people* for a while and eventually settled on *folks*, which felt more inclusive to me. By the time I started using that term on a regular basis, it made a lot of sense to me. Over time, the three of us began to focus in on other gender issues in the classroom as well.

It is interesting that some of my most vulnerable moments have come in recent months, years into our project. Publishing articles is very exciting for me, but it increases my vulnerability as well. Once the tools we had been developing to analyze our data had become more sophisticated, they began revealing more detailed findings. The power of the magnification increased, and, as Jerri says, I saw things that did not match my beliefs or my image of myself as a teacher. Then my anxiety increased as well. But we kept talking and continued analyzing and clarifying our findings. I was able to trust that what I had perceived at first as my worst moments of teaching could be made public because the stories were told with honesty and lots and lots of thought and talk. Jerri and her colleague had become a part of the classroom, too. They acknowledged that some of the things that I had not realized about the students were things that they had not seen, either. So we all began to look further at what we had missed and to consider why we had missed it. I think going through that anxiety actually moved our work to a new level, and I was able to see a broader purpose for it. I'm less concerned now about readers' reactions to how I acted or failed to act in a particular situation on a particular day.

I enjoy being a member of our research team. We negotiate a lot. In our writing, one person usually takes the lead, but then we all read it and meet and discuss it in detail. We read multiple drafts and all have extensive input. We also continue to refine our tools and procedures, and we realize that these tools will bring tensions to the surface. But within our group, we bring the tensions to a safe place where we can examine them.

When teachers begin to value research, teaching gets exciting. My hope for the future is that more small professional development schools in this country will enable researchers to build long-term relationships with a small group of teachers. I imagine these schools as settings where asking questions about our practice and ourselves as teachers is an integral part of the culture. I envision these schools as places that are safe enough to allow the tensions and joys of such work to surface.

REFERENCES

Brown, A. (1992). Design experiments: Theoretical and methodological challenges in creating complex interventions in classroom settings. *The Journal of the Learning Sciences, 2*, 148–178.

Caulk, N. (1996). *Exploring the teacher/researcher communication gap.* Unpublished master's thesis, School for International Training, Brattleboro, VT.

Irujo, S. (1998). *Teaching bilingual children: Beliefs and behaviors.* Boston: Heinle & Heinle.

Kennedy, M. (1997). The connection between research and practice. *Educational Researcher, 26*(7), 4–12.

Wilson-Keenan, J., Willett, J., & Solsken, J. (1993). Focus on research: Constructing an urban village: School/home collaboration in a multicultural classroom. *Language Arts, 70*, 204–214.

PROMOTING FURTHER CONVERSATIONS

Beyer, L. (1988). *Knowing and acting: Inquiry, ideology, and educational studies.* London: Falmer.

Cochran-Smith, M., & Lytle, S. (1993). *Inside/outside: Teacher research and knowledge.* New York: Teacher's College Press.

Freeman, D. (1996). Redefining the relationship between research and what teachers know. In K. Bailey & D. Nunan (Eds.), *Voices from the language classroom* (pp. 88–115). Cambridge, England: Cambridge University Press.

Gallas, K. (2001). Teachers' knowledge and children's lives: Loose change in the battle for educational currency. *Language Arts, 78*, 570–574.

Hawkins, M., & Legler, L. (2004). Reflections on the impact of teacher-researcher collaboration. *TESOL Quarterly, 38*, 339–343.

Closely Examined Work: An Epilogue To The LTEC Conversations

Donald Freeman

An Uneasy Balance

A great deal has been written recently about the importance of collaborative inquiry in education (Darling-Hammond, 1998; Darling-Hammond & Sykes, 1999). Whether such inquiry is undertaken among students, teachers (Hawley & Valli, 1999), or indeed among teacher educators (Johnson, 2000), inquiry and collaboration are deemed important to the learning process. In one sense, however, they make strange companions.

Inquiry involves closely examining the work one is doing and how one is doing it to better understand, and perhaps redirect, the outcomes (Freeman, 1998). Inquiry might start with a question, or perhaps not. But at its heart, the process stems from a sense of unsureness, of wondering if (and how) the assumptions one is making might be mistaken (Duckworth, 1987). Thus, what drives inquiry is this feeling of being off balance. Because it can create a sense of vulnerability, inquiry is not usually associated with social interaction or with the culture of schools. Best to be private about what one is unsure of, or so the feeling goes, rather than share it with the world. This is particularly the case in education, where the culture of schools insists—both tacitly and explicitly—that getting things right is what matters (McDonald, 1992).

While inquiry can be entirely individual and private, collaboration introduces social interaction. Collaboration, where people work together toward some common end, suggests a lack of formal hierarchy among the players, a sense of mutual openness to the ideas and proposals of others, and an element of shared purpose. Thus collaboration places inquiry in a social medium, with all the risks inherent in going public. It also brings the need to use language together. As people collaborate, they talk with or write to one another. This process of putting thoughts into words, of articulating thoughts, questions, and ideas to others, creates an opportunity to hear oneself think out loud (Freeman, 1998). So these two processes exist in an uneasy balance. Inquiry hinges on wonder and a lack of certainty, while collaboration depends on articulating what one thinks one knows.

All of which is well and good on an abstract level. However, although proponents of collaborative inquiry argue for this process in education, there are few examples of what it actually looks like in practice, particularly among teacher educators, which is why this book is an exception. The conversations in this book show collaborative inquiry in action among a group of language teacher educators. Both the content and the process of the conversations provide us with insights and examples of what it means to closely examine the work of ESOL teacher education. My aim, then, is to provide observations about the uneasy balance intrinsic to collaborative inquiry. My comments are organized around four themes that coalesce out of the preceding chapters: joining the teaching club, authority and control, the facts of the (subject) matter, and using knowledge. These themes, which I have purposely labeled in a rather telegraphic way, capture some of the core issues that scaffold the work in teacher education. So in the spirit of T. S. Eliot (1968, p. 47), that "the end of all our exploring / Will be to arrive where we started / And know the place for the first time," this conclusion offers an epilogue of sorts and the beginning to further conversations.

Joining The Teaching Club

Early on in these conversations, the central question of learning and belonging is introduced. Francis Bailey presents the challenge rather starkly:

> I think we have to abandon this idea that teachers can learn to teach from our courses. They're not going to get skills from sitting in our classes. They're going to encounter certain kinds of questions current in the field. . . . They can test things out on themselves, but ultimately they're not going to learn to teach in our classrooms. (this volume, p. 27)

Bailey's comment, and indeed the whole first chapter, poses this critical question of how people learn to teach second language learners in class-rooms. In the conversation, we introduce questions of teacher learning, the role of knowledge (sometimes referred to in these conversations as "decontextualized hard facts," this volume, p. 29), and community in the professional training of teachers. The discussion frames two perhaps overly dichotomous positions. Teachers are either made through the knowledge and skills they acquire and possess, or they are born out of the classroom situations in which they find themselves. This classic dilemma about the roots of teaching knowledge draws a contrast at the most fundamental level between epistemology—it's what teachers know that defines their work—and ontology—it's who teachers are and what they do that defines that work.

Beyond the usual philosophy of the made-versus-born debate, these two positions mark the extremes of a professional learning continuum. As poles of that continuum, each one is both problematic and illuminating. To critique direct instruction in the professional knowledge base by arguing, or admitting, as Bailey puts it, that participants are "not going to learn to teach in our teacher education classrooms" can be taken either as an abdication of the role and responsibility of the teacher educator or as a frank recognition of the basic truth of the situation. However, to say that new teachers learn only through working in classrooms is to argue for an extended craft model, which risks simply replicating existing classroom practices as good (or poor) as they are in that particular context.

We find these positions in the present debates over teacher quality, as expressed in notions of standardized knowledge and professional socialization (see Cochran-Smith & Fries, 2001). Arguments that favor the knowledge base of teaching hold that professional standards will improve teaching and learning, while arguments that favor socialization contend that site-based support, such as new teacher mentoring, is central to effective teacher learning. These macro debates, and indeed the dichotomy between knowledge and socialization in teacher learning, or what Wallace (1991) called the applied science versus the craft models of teacher training, obscure a more basic pattern. How do teacher learners access and use information in their professional learning? How do they, as teacher-respondent Tom Nicoletti puts it, "become part of the conversation"? How do they join the teaching club?

This question of professional entry, of learning the rules of the conversation, raises the contrast of what is tacit and what can be explicit in this process of learning to teach. Tacitness and explicitness cut across these positions of knowledge versus socialization as a sort of yin and yang. For example, in a teacher education methods class, teacher learners work explicitly on how to teach, how to present content, how to group students, how to assess their progress with the language, and so on. Explicit knowledge and skills are introduced, practiced, and likely critiqued. Professional learning is clearly taking place within a setting: the university seminar room or lecture hall in the teacher education context. It is also taking place within a web of defined social relationships: between teacher educator and teacher learner and among teacher learners themselves. So tacit aspects of socialization are definitely at work, even though the methods class seems to focus on the explicit information and skills being "taught."

Shift the venue to the school, perhaps during a practicum or the first year of teaching. In this setting, the social roles are explicit: the cooperating teacher, a mentor teacher perhaps, and the novice teacher. There may be a university-based teacher educator as well. These roles define and shape who does what, who can comment on or critique whom, and which practices or ways of doing things are valued. The roles depend on, and actually exemplify, tacit aspects of knowledge in the particular classroom situation: knowledge from experience, knowledge (or lack of it) that stems from identity (the race, gender, social class of the teachers and students), as well as the tacit norms of activity and curriculum.

In the first instance, the teacher education methods class, the knowledge and skills are explicit, while the socialization is implicit. In the second, the practicum or early years of teaching, the roles and socialization are explicit, while the knowledge is more tacit. Yet in both cases, the explicit and the tacit combine in professional learning.

So joining the teaching club, like learning to read or other social practices (Lave, 1997; Lave & Wenger, 1991), involves navigating this complex traffic pattern of explicit and tacit knowledge. As a postulant teacher (Berliner, 1998), you have to balance what you are told to do with what you figure out and how it makes sense to you. Either one alone will not complete the picture. Tom Nicoletti, the new teacher who comments in the first chapter, frames the question in terms of two vivid metaphors: "Do we view . . . advances in our knowledge as though they were bricks being added to the edifice of Education?" Or are they "all just part of a 'conversation' about how we think things work" (this volume, p. 29)? It is likely a bit of both. Brick by brick or turn by turn, something is being done and there are rules by which to do it. To me, the question hinges on how we, as teacher educators, organize and orchestrate access to these rules of the teaching game. It is less a matter of where and how these rules, be they knowledge or social roles, are encountered, in the university or the school, than a matter of what information is learnable within those settings.

Authority and Control: Who Knows What?

The second theme addresses the issue of authority and what constitutes teaching knowledge. What makes someone an authority on classroom teaching? Is it knowledge? Experience? Or some hybrid of both? This theme echoes the knowledge-versus-socialization dilemma, but the tension is phrased in terms of expert knowledge versus experience. The conversation moves beyond this dichotomous frame to examine how professional development connects with and moves between so-called expert knowledge, which is external to the school setting, and the participating teachers' rich and varied experiences.

Jerri Willett introduces a useful way to think about the structure of in-service professional development as a potential platform for engaging expert knowledge with experience. Commenting on state-mandated requirements that can shape professional development, Willett says, "Rather than seeing the structure . . . as a problem, we could explore how to persuade teachers to look at things differently. . . . You use the authority of the structure to create a space for persuasion" (this volume, p. 38). This notion of structure as space intrigues me. Clearly the structures of schools, teacher education, and professional development, though distinctive, share many attributes. Perhaps key among them is the idea that authority depends on (and comes from) expert knowledge.

The role of the teacher (or teacher educator or staff developer) as knower, as expert, organizes educational structures. Teachers are thus evaluated on their subject-matter knowledge; teacher education programs are organized around academic disciplines for content and education courses for teaching methods; and professional development often consists of presenters external to the school talking about new content or practices. Much of this structure can lead to the notion of education as transmission. To counter this fundamental design, teachers may restructure their classrooms to make them student or learning centered (e.g., as in cooperative learning, Montessori, or Summerhill). Teacher educators may restructure their courses to negotiate the content or syllabus (as discussed in chapter 3). And professional development may be restructured to make it more participatory or collaborative. Reorganize as we will, however, "the authority of the structure" of teacher expertise (to use Willett's phrase) persists, as a kind of Chomskyan deep structure, in the work of education.

The problem with this deep structure is not that it exists, but rather that it creates (or contributes to) a deficit design in teaching and learning at all levels. The teacher knows; the students don't know. The teacher educator has the content and skills; the teacher learners need to acquire them. The staff developer has expertise; the teachers don't. To counter this deficit design, people argue in favor of the learners, for what learners, at all levels, bring to learning. Broadly put, this is the core of the constructivist philosophy: Learners possess experiences and expertise that they use to build new knowledge and understanding. How they actually do so is a matter of debate and experimentation. Ironically, however, arguing for what learners know and bring to the table in teaching and learning still operates from the deficit design's deep structure. It simply shifts the balance by saying that learners have some experience or expertise of their own out of which they themselves can fill the deficit. So learning still involves filling deficits; the constructivist approach just changes who does the filling.

But it strikes me that this argument about whether learners know nothing or have something, this dichotomy between transmission and constructivism, is misplaced. Rather, these deep structures create spaces of possibility. Ken Pransky in his response points out the dilemma that, on the one hand, participation breeds ownership, while, on the other, development and change often require outsiders' nonparticipatory perspectives. Regarding the former, Pransky says, "When administration approaches teachers supportively, as competent professionals, and asks them to analyze student needs, . . . most teachers will respond in kind" (this volume, p. 51). Regarding the latter, he also points out, as a teacher, that "some school systems engage in numerous questionable practices with uniformly poor educational results. . . . Administrators have a responsibility to the students to insist on whatever training they believe their staff needs" (p. 50). In the latter instance, the fact of in-service training or professional development creates what Willett calls the "space for persuasion." The ends are clear—to improve schools on behalf of students—but how that space is actually manipulated to achieve those ends is the challenge of effective professional development.

Orienting teacher education and professional development away from who knows what and toward what needs to be done shifts the notion of authority. It no longer depends on a deficit in the student or in the teacher learner. The aim is no longer to transmit, to fill that deficit with knowledge and skills, or to construct understandings until that deficit is repaired; rather, authority turns on participants' perceptions, practices, and ways of ascertaining learning. For students, authority comes through recognizing and managing their own learning, a process that we sometimes call *learner autonomy*. For teachers, authority comes from two interrelated sources: their ability to recognize and respond to learning in the students they are teaching, and their simultaneous capacity to recognize and manage their own professional learning.

The Facts of the (Subject) Matter and How to Package Them

Understanding learning on all these various levels—student learning in the classroom, teacher learning in professional preparation and staff development, even organizational learning in school reform—is a central challenge that these conversations returned to over and over again. But learning what? What is the object of learning? The third theme examines this question of what language teachers in particular know, and need to know, about their content. What is it that makes someone a language teacher, as contrasted perhaps with a speaker or user of the language? The discussions about content in chapters 4 and 5 raise interesting issues in response. These questions are not new, however. Some in TESOL have argued that specific and articulated knowledge of language, through applied linguistics for example, provides the sine qua non for language teachers (e.g., Muchisky & Yates, 2001). This line of thinking has been extended to posit that language teachers are unique and differ from other teachers because of their subject matter (Tarone & Allwright, 2001). But it strikes me that these debates, in which I too have participated, probably miss the point. Clearly, language teachers need to have subject matter[1] that they prepare and teach. The question is not whether that subject matter is important (it is), or whether that subject matter is unique (a harder question to answer), but rather how that subject matter comes about both in the classroom and in the professional world (Freeman & Johnson, 1998). How is language as subject matter created in professional training, and how is it used to teach in foreign or second language classrooms? On this point, the LTEC conversations make a useful contribution.

Three key questions frame their contribution: What are the "facts" of language? Does it make sense to distinguish between knowledge of language and its uses (in our case, in classrooms)? And is there something unique about language as classroom content? In addressing these questions, LTEC members thread issues of power and access throughout the discussions. This perspective moves the conversation beyond the argument or contention that language teachers are different. Within a perspective of power and access, one recognizes that not only is language arbitrary, as de Saussure (1978) made clear, but also that labels about language— metalanguage—are equally arbitrary. Thus conventional categories of language analysis such as nouns and verbs, or the present perfect or modal verbs, are all products of a point of view. They are how someone sees language. This positioning of knowledge in no way trivializes or even relativizes it. It simply applies a level of theoretical consistency.

---

[1] I am distinguishing here, as Karen Johnson and I have done (Freeman & Johnson, 1998, p. 410ff), between *subject matter* and *content:* Subject matter refers to the broad range of knowledge and skills, often discipline based or discipline derived, that makes up an area of study; content refers to how that subject matter is instantiated in a particular activity, lesson, or course.

Playing out this line of thinking reveals that the privilege of naming these categories as *the facts of the language* creates a sense of ownership and control. In our field of English language teaching, we could say that applied linguistics has created a democratic form of access to these facts of the English language. Anyone can study them; anyone can learn them; indeed anyone can use (or misuse) them. Counterpoised to this democracy of access through the study of applied linguistics is the profoundly undemocratic illusion of the "native speaker" of a language, which turns on the idea that somehow birth and upbringing, rather than learning, create linguistic fluency. Much excellent work has been done to problematize this notion of the native speaker (e.g., Braine, 1999), but it nevertheless remains a powerful discriminator.

In many ways, this tension between equal access to naming the facts of the language through applied linguistics, on the one hand, and the privileging myth of the native speaker, on the other, lies at the heart of our struggles with subject matter in language teaching. Put simply, is it knowledge of the language that matters most, or is it use? The discussions in chapter 4, however, raise a different dimension of the same issue. Central to language teaching is the idea that knowledge of the language drives its use. Therefore, students study forms of the language—dialogues, verb tenses, vocabulary lists—to improve how they use the language. The problem with this notion is that knowledge and use are so interconnected as to be almost inextricable. As de Saussure (1978) argued in distinguishing between *langue,* or language, and *parole,* or speaking, and as Chomsky (1968) proposed in distinguishing performance from competence, knowledge is abstract, acontextual, and in that sense invisible, while use is concrete, contexted, and in that sense visible or audible.

For teachers, the LTEC discussants' promotion of naming language facts has a generative quality that is critical to teaching and to teacher knowledge. Kathleen Graves argues this generative approach when she says,

> In a linguistics course, you're not just teaching [teachers] facts so they can go and look things up in a reference grammar. The challenge is what they do with that knowledge. They're not linguists, they're not grammarians, that's not the purpose of it. The purpose is to give them tools to be able to investigate the language. Why and

> how are they going to use the tools when they teach? (this volume,
> p. 81)

Thus, knowledge of language is tied to how the teacher uses it in planning and carrying out instruction. This idea raises the question of pedagogical content knowledge (chapter 5). Is classroom teachers' knowledge of language a subset of full metalinguistic knowledge? Or is it somehow distinct because teachers develop it by using and applying it in and through classroom interactions? The position that teachers' knowledge of language is a subset of full knowledge casts teachers as partial knowers of what linguists know. Thus, for language teachers who are not teaching their mother tongue (however it may be defined), this creates a sort of double jeopardy. The language as content is not fully yours and neither is linguistic knowledge. Perhaps this double jeopardy explains why so-called nonnative teachers are often very passionate in their pursuit of descriptive linguistic knowledge. It pits the more democratic access to knowledge available through applied linguistics against the privileging myth of the native speaker and linguistic birthright.

On the level of instruction, this issue of knowledge versus use of language is primarily a question of packaging. How is this subject matter packaged into classroom content? For students in second or foreign language classrooms, knowledge equals use: Students learn from what they and/or their teachers use in class. Which is not to say that everything that is used is learned; rather, it is a question of availability. The language used in the classroom becomes available to be worked with and perhaps learned. But if it is not used, then how can that part of the language be available? I remember a clear instance of this principle of availability when I was learning French in secondary school. Although the classes were language rich, taught entirely in the target language using the audiovisual method, we never encountered the French one would use for talking to babies and very young children. In the summer of my third year, I worked on a farm in central France, in a family with two young children. Although I could survive in most situations with adults, I was tongue-tied and indeed incomprehensible to the 3-year-old and the 5-year-old. A few weeks of listening in on their mother as she went about her daily caregiving eventually enabled me to interact with them in some ways and to make myself understood.

Of course, many other language domains are similarly out of reach to usual classroom instruction. Perhaps ironically, the language of classroom management often presents a similar challenge to teachers who while growing up were not schooled in the language they are teaching. So these teachers may use their mother tongue, the one in which they themselves were schooled, to manage their classes even as they are teaching the second language as content. This is not a critique. It simply confirms this availability principle, namely that the language used in the classroom becomes available to be learned. The issue is, of course, how that language is used. How is it packaged in that classroom? Is it packaged in interaction, group work, cooperative activities, or in teacher-fronted exercises, lectures, and work sheets, or a combination? Learning the language depends in part on how it is used, how it is made available in the classroom. This availability determines how subject matter becomes content. And it depends in large measure on the teacher.

Using Knowledge in Teaching/to Teach

Knowledge, and how it is used in teaching, is the fourth and last theme in this epilogical analysis. For me, this issue is at the heart of closely examining teacher education practices. Once one steps away from the transfer metaphor that dominates most of the policy, public rhetoric, and even practices in educating teachers (Freeman & Johnson, 1998), one comes face-to-face with questions about the types of knowledge and knowing that teaching involves. What are they? How do they relate to one another? How do they interact? Where does teaching knowledge come from and how is it used? The response can certainly be that these are big questions (which they are) that are not easily addressed or resolved (which is true). And in the final analysis, how much do they actually matter to the doing of classroom teaching?

Actually, I think that these questions probably matter very little to classroom teaching. I do not mean that they are unimportant but simply that teaching is, can be, and will be done without much reflective analysis on the underpinnings of the work. As Caleb Gattegno has observed on many occasions, teaching involves turning time into experience. There are myriad ways to work that conversion in the language classroom, some of which may work better than others. But on the level of classroom teaching, the driving questions are not about teacher knowledge; they are—or should be—about student learning: What are my students learning? How are they learning it? How do I, as teacher, know? What evidence or data do I have of their learning? Where and how can I locate that evidence? How do I (re)adjust my instruction based on this evidence? These are technical questions in the very best sense of the word. They are questions that skip over issues of what language teachers know and go quickly to what they do with that knowledge.

In contrast, questions of teacher knowledge do seem to me central to the work of teacher educators. Indeed, the six conversations in this book each probe in different ways issues of what teacher learners need to know to do their work effectively. The conversation on the role of research (chapter 6) brings these ruminations together in an interesting way. As with the preceding discussions, this one contains many familiar threads. There is the question of purpose: Who is research for? If it is for teachers as practitioners, then shouldn't teachers play a much more central role in defining questions and the value of findings? There is the question of distance and location: How can work done in one setting influence practices in another? How can the perspectives of those who are outside the classroom ecology, such as researchers, usefully inform the inhabitants of those ecologies?

There are questions of ultimate use: What is the aim of the undertaking? Francis Bailey captures this last question when he observes that many educational researchers, like the LTEC discussants, are "oriented toward . . . very thick descriptions of classrooms" (this volume, p. 108). Thus they try to render the specifics of the time, place, and participation in that one setting as closely as they can. This localness is, however, opposite to what teachers as potential users of that research might be looking for: They want to know how the information relates to their own work and classrooms. As Bailey says, "Teachers must wonder, 'How does this generalize to my case?'" (p. 108). So while researchers look to open-ended uses of analyses drawn from specific contexts, teachers look for specific uses of analyses played out in the open-endedness of day-to-day teaching. "I wonder if that open-endedness isn't one of the things that makes research very difficult for teachers to relate to," Bailey concludes (p. 108). Maybe so. Or perhaps it has to do with contrapuntal forms of open-endedness. The researcher, who often bases statements on limited settings and data, strives to curtail generalization and leave such statements open-ended, whereas the teacher, who engages with students and their learning in an open-ended way, can use general statements to guide particular actions.

At its essence, I think this is the core tension of using knowledge in teaching. It is the job, and even one might argue the responsibility, of teacher educators and educational researchers to create maps—theories, principles, teaching methods, forms of linguistic analysis, and so on—that can serve to guide learners of teaching. These maps come from specific territories; they are drawn in reference to people and events in classrooms. But by their function as maps they lose that particularity on which they are based. So as maps, they become knowledge, of teaching methods, applied linguistics, language learning strategies, and so on. This is knowledge that teacher educators use to do their work. We are working cartographers. We argue about the accuracy of our maps, about the scales of representation on them (are they too fine or too broad?), about the faithfulness of the mapmaking processes used to create them (is there adequate triangulation?). As teacher educators, we also guide newcomers into the territory of teaching by helping them to use these maps to locate themselves and where they want to go. In some instances, we also show them how to make their own maps.

The learner or doer of teaching, however, inhabits a different world when it comes to using this knowledge. The map may show a road, the next unit of the curriculum for instance, but the teacher knows that the road has been washed out by last week's flood of prevacation activities, and that it will not be traversable until things settle down and the waters recede. So the teacher's use of the knowledge centers on how she maps now into tomorrow, next week, and even into the end of the school year. She uses the maps to turn students' time into experience. Just as a cartographer and a traveler have different but interrelated purposes, so too do teacher educator and teacher. They both deal with the landscape of student learning, but they have different responsibilities in that landscape. The teacher educator–cartographer can prepare and offer maps; the teacher-traveler uses those maps.

This parallelism might seem simple, were it not for another level, one that often confounds the first. In addition to their roles as cartographers, teacher educators are also teachers; they teach teachers. So as teachers, teacher educators use maps to guide their travels in the landscape of teacher learning. This, it seems to me, is where things become messy. The maps of teacher learning are relatively new and incomplete at best. Teacher educators have traveled much over the years, but they have mapped very little of the terrain that they inhabit and through which they move. Teacher educator Ken Zeichner summed up the situation in his 1998 vice-presidential address to the Division on Teaching and Teacher Education of the American Educational Research Association. Commenting on teacher education research, Zeichner (1999) observed,

> Although there were hundreds of studies reported which sought to assess the impact of training teachers to do particular things, very few researchers actually looked at the process of teacher education as it happened over time and at how teachers and student teachers interpreted and gave meaning to the preservice and professional development programs they experienced. (p. 5)

All of which brings us full circle to the work of the LTEC group. This group has begun to look at the processes of second language teacher education and, to borrow Zeichner's words, at how learners of teaching have given meaning to the preservice and professional development programs they have experienced. I believe that one small group of teacher educators scrutinizing their own work accomplishes many things. As we said in the introduction, it provides a possible model of a process. It also provides one group's contribution to mapping this territory of teacher learning in the field of TESOL. Perhaps it is also a travel narrative of the mapmaking. If it does only these things, then LTEC has rendered a useful service.

REFERENCES

Berliner, D. (1998). *The development of expertise in teaching.* Washington, DC: AACTE.

Braine, G. (Ed). (1999). *Non-native educators in English language teaching.* Mahwah, NJ: Lawrence Erlbaum.

Chomsky, N. (1968). *Language and mind.* New York: Harcourt.

Cochran-Smith, M., & Fries, M. K. (2001). Sticks, stones, and ideology: The discourse of reform in teacher education. *Educational Researcher, 30*(8), 3–15.

Darling-Hammond, L. (1998). Teachers and teaching: Testing policy hypotheses from a National Commission Report. *Educational Researcher, 27*(1), 5–15.

Darling-Hammond, L., & Sykes, G. (Eds.). (1999). *Teaching as a learning profession: Handbook of policy and practice.* San Francisco: Jossey-Bass.

de Saussure, F. (1978). *A course in general linguistics.* Glasgow, Scotland: Collins.

Duckworth, E. (1987). The virtues of not knowing. In E. Duckworth, *The having of wonderful ideas and other essays on teaching and learning* (pp. 64–69). New York: Teachers College Press.

Eliot, T. S. (1968). *Four quartets: Little Gidding V.* London: Harvest Books.

Freeman, D. (1998). *Doing teacher-research: From inquiry to understanding.* Boston: Heinle & Heinle.

Freeman, D., & Johnson, K. E. (1998). Reconceptualizing the knowledge-base of language teacher education. *TESOL Quarterly, 32,* 397–417.

Hawley, W., & Valli, L. (1999). The essentials of effective professional development: A new consensus. In L. Darling-Hammond & G. Sykes (Eds.), *Teaching and the learning profession: Handbook of policy and practice* (pp. 127–150). San Francisco: Jossey-Bass.

Johnson, K. E. (Ed.). (2000). *Case studies in TESOL teacher education.* Alexandria, VA: TESOL.

Lave, J. (1997). The culture of acquisition and the practice of understanding. In D. Kirshner & J. A. Whitson (Eds.), *Situated cognition: Social, semiotic, and psychological perspectives* (pp. 17–35). Mahwah, NJ: Lawrence Erlbaum.

Lave, J., & Wenger, E. (1991). *Situated learning: Legitimate peripheral participation.* New York: Cambridge University Press.

McDonald, J. (1992). *Teaching: Making sense of an uncertain craft.* New York: Teachers College Press.

Muchisky, D., & Yates, R. (2001, March). *On reconceptualizing teacher education research.* Paper presented at the 35th Annual TESOL Convention, St Louis, MO.

Tarone, E., & Allwright, D. (2001, May). *Language teacher-learning and student language-learning: Shaping the knowledge-base.* Paper presented at the Second International Conference on Second Language Teacher Education, University of Minnesota, Minneapolis, MN.

Wallace, M. (1991). *Training foreign language teachers: A reflective approach.* Cambridge, England: Cambridge University Press.

Zeichner, K. (1999). The new scholarship in teacher education. *Educational Researcher, 28*(2), 4–15.

Contributors

Francis Bailey is an associate professor of language teacher education at the School for International Training in Brattleboro, Vermont, in the United States. His research interests include issues of home and school compatibility and methods for helping culturally and linguistically diverse students learn more effectively in mainstream school environments.

Amy Powell Faeskorn teaches ESL in the Boston Public Schools in Boston, Massachusetts, in the United States. She has taught ESOL to adults in the United States, Ecuador, and Morocco, and holds a master of arts in teaching from the School for International Training in Brattleboro, Vermont, in the United States.

Avrom Feinberg is the program director for the Rocky Mountain Youth Corps in Steamboat Springs, Colorado, in the United States. He wrote his contribution to this volume shortly after he completed a master's in education at the Boston University program in Quito, Ecuador, where he taught English and social studies to international sixth-grade students at the Colegio Menor San Francisco de Quito.

Donald Freeman is dean of graduate and professional studies in language teacher education and director of the Center for Teacher Education, Training, and Research at the School for International Training in Brattleboro, Vermont, in the United States. In teaching, research, and program design, his work focuses on how teachers develop and change their understandings of what they do.

Kathleen Graves is an associate professor of language teacher education and chair of the academic year master of arts in teaching at the School for International Training in Brattleboro, Vermont, in the United States. A former chair of the TESOL Publications Committee, she consults internationally on language curriculum design and teacher education.

Margaret Hawkins is an assistant professor in the Department of Curriculum and Instruction at the University of Wisconsin at Madison, in the United States, where she directs the ESL and bilingual certification and graduate programs. Her research interests include literacies and sociolinguistics, focusing on young English language learners in schools and on language teacher education.

Suzanne Irujo is a professor emerita of education at Boston University in Boston, Massachusetts, in the United States, and a visiting professor at the University of Wisconsin at Madison in the United States. Before retiring, she was a teacher and teacher educator in ESL, EFL, bilingual education, and foreign language education. Since retiring, she stays busy writing, consulting, and developing materials in those fields.

Jo-Anne Wilson Keenan is an elementary school principal and teacher in Springfield, Massachusetts, in the United States, and a research team member at the University of Massachusetts at Amherst. She is also the program director of the Springfield Learning Community Collaborative, a partnership of teachers, students, families, and the university designed to change relationships between urban families and schools.

Diane Larsen-Freeman is a professor of education, professor of linguistics, and the director of the English Language Institute at the University of

Michigan at Ann Arbor, in the United States, and a distinguished senior faculty fellow at the School for International Training in Brattleboro, Vermont, in the United States. She has spoken and published widely on teacher education, second language acquisition, English grammar, and language teaching methodology.

Tom Nicoletti earned his master's of education in TESOL at the University of Massachusetts at Amherst, in the United States. Since then, he has been teaching EFL at the National Pingtung Teachers College in Taiwan, People's Republic of China, where he enjoys helping students prepare to become elementary school English teachers.

Ken Pransky teaches ESL at an elementary school in Amherst, Massachusetts, in the United States. He has worked in multicultural education for 30 years, teaching students of all ages as well as adults in the United States, Iran, Japan, Spain, and Mexico. He is interested in classroom-based research and in the role that culture plays in learning.

Ellen Rintell is a professor of education at Salem State College in Salem, Massachusetts, in the United States, where she is co-coordinator of the master of arts in teaching ESL program. A former ESL and bilingual education teacher, she is interested in teacher education, especially preparing bilingual paraprofessionals to become teachers of English language learners.

Ellie Schmitt teaches ESL in an elementary school in Madison, Wisconsin, in the United States. She holds a master's degree from the University of Wisconsin at Madison in curriculum and instruction with a focus on ESL. Ellie has traveled extensively and speaks both German and Indonesian.

Jerri Willett is a professor at the University of Massachusetts at Amherst in the United States. She is currently participating in a dialogic inquiry-based project with local educators to study their collective and critical responses to shifting institutional policies and discourses around English language learners on the nature and consequences of classroom practices.

Also Available From TESOL

Academic Writing Programs
Ilona Leki, Editor

Action Research
Julian Edge, Editor

Bilingual Education
Donna Christian and Fred Genesee, Editors

Community Partnerships
Elsa Auerbach, Editor

Content-Based Instruction in Higher Education Settings
JoAnn Crandell and Dorit Kaufman, Editors

Distance-Learning Programs
Lynn E. Henrichsen, Editor

English for Specific Purposes
Thomas Orr, Editor

Gender and English Language Learners
Bonny Norton and Aneta Pavlenko, Editors

Grammar Teaching in Teacher Education
Dilin Liu and Peter Master, Editors

Implementing the ESL Standards for Pre-K–12 Students Through Teacher Education
Marguerite Ann Snow, Editor

Integrating the ESL Standards Into Classroom Practice: Grades Pre-K–2
Betty Ansin Smallwood, Editor

Integrating the ESL Standards Into Classroom Practice: Grades 6–8
Suzanne Irujo, Editor

Integrating the ESL Standards Into Classroom Practice: Grades 9–12
Barbara Agor, Editor

Intensive English Programs in Postsecondary Settings
Nicholas Dimmit and Maria Dantas-Whitney, Editors

Interaction and Language Learning
Jill Burton and Charles Clennell, Editors

Internet for English Teaching
Mark Warschauer, Heidi Shetzer, and Christine Meloni

Journal Writing
Jill Burton and Michael Carroll, Editors

Mainstreaming
Effie Cochran, Editor

Teacher Education
Karen E. Johnson, Editor

Technology-Enhanced Learning Environments
Elizabeth Hanson-Smith, Editor

For more information, contact
Teachers of English to Speakers of Other Languages, Inc.
700 South Washington Street, Suite 200
Alexandria, Virginia 22314 USA
Tel 703-836-0774 • Fax 703-836-6447 • publications@tesol.org •
http://www.tesol.org/